Did you ever wonder what US taxpayers spent their money on during the Cold War? Frederic Hunter has created a delicious take down of the US Foreign Service that reads like Carl Hiaasen.

Hunter's tale is rollicking, ribald, and also nuanced and elegiac. Beneath the comedy show of Cold War diplomacy, he has written a love song to a rich land and sweet people in a moment of quiet before the storm.

 —Scott C. Davis, *The Road from Damascus*

A colorful mosaic of history, politics, and personal experience in the Congo. Fred Hunter's *Kivu* recreates the chaotic years following independence from Belgium in 1960. A young USIS officer arriving three years later, Hunter was assigned to the Eastern district of Kivu—by comparison, a paradise amidst the disorder. He brings to life an intriguing group of Congolese, Belgians, and Americans who survive—and savor—this lost time with hope, love, and sorrow.

 —Jinny Webber, *Bedtrick,* and *The Secret Player*

Frederic Hunter's writing on Africa makes old Africa hands want to drop everything and head back for the life of daily adventure Hunter depicts so well. Newcomers to the continent will find insight to help them face its many enigmas.

 —Richard Matheron, former US Ambassador to Swaziland

Frederic Hunter's memoir *Kivu* is an entertaining read about an isolated district in the eastern Congo in 1963, soon after independence. A new foreign service officer fresh from training, Hunter set forth to bring American culture to the jungle. Pitted against the guns and cash of our adversaries in the Cold War, Fred gave numerous Show and Tell presentations about life in America, "So they would like us."

Gradually, Hunter shed his innocence as he learned to read the subtleties and nuances of political and cultural power. He encountered a flamboyant African king, grasping Congolese politicians, and expatriates—some devoted to service, the others, well, not so much.

A birds-eye view of the Congo at a crossroads in history.
—Gretchen McCullough, *Confessions of a Knight Errant*

Frederic Hunter, our literary guide to what Europeans long referred to as the "dark continent," opens a window and lets in the light. In the aftermath of independence in 1960, Congo was buffeted by chaos and carnage. Yet, as Hunter explains, the sublime lakeside district of Kivu was largely untouched, fragile, a perfect world.

Here we meet the good-natured locals, an international crew of diplomats scheming on behalf of their governments, lining up amorous adventures, or, like Hunter himself, just happy to have this fleeting taste of paradise.
—Stephen Fife, *Loving Holly*

KIVU

**Journeys Through
Eastern Congo in a
Time of Rebellion & Cold War**

Frederic Hunter

Cune

Kivu:
Journeys Through Eastern Congo
in a Time of Rebellion and Cold War
Frederic Hunter
© 2022 Frederic Hunter
Cune Press, Seattle 2022
First Edition

Paperback   ISBN 9781951082031 $16.00

Please contact us for Catalog in Publication info:
www.cunepress.com

For the Mesa Writers

I would like to thank my wife Donanne, my son Paul, and
the crew at Cune Press for their help in bringing this book
into being.
—Frederic Hunter

Note on Naming:
This book concerns the Democratic Republic of the Congo, some-
times referred to as Congo-Kinshasa, DR Congo, the DRC, the
DROC or the Congo (before 1997 called "Zaire").

Bridge Between the Cultures (a series from Cune Press)

Afghanistan & Beyond	Linda Sartor
Congo Prophet	Frederic Hunter
Confessions of a Knight Errant	Gretchen McCullough
Empower a Refugee	Patricia Martin Holt
Nietzsche Awakens!	Farid Younes
Stories My Father Told Me	Helen Zughaib, Elia Zughaib
Apartheid is a Crime	Mats Svensson
Arab Boy Delivered	Paul Aziz Zarou

Syria Crossroads (a series from Cune Press)

The Dusk Visitor	Musa Al-Halool
White Carnations	MusaRahum Abbas
East of the Grand Umayyad	Sami Moubayed
The Road from Damascus	Scott C. Davis
A Pen of Damascus Steel	Ali Ferzat
Jinwar and Other Stories	Alex Poppe

Cune Cune Press: www.cunepress.com | www.cunepress.net

Contents

Table of Illustrations

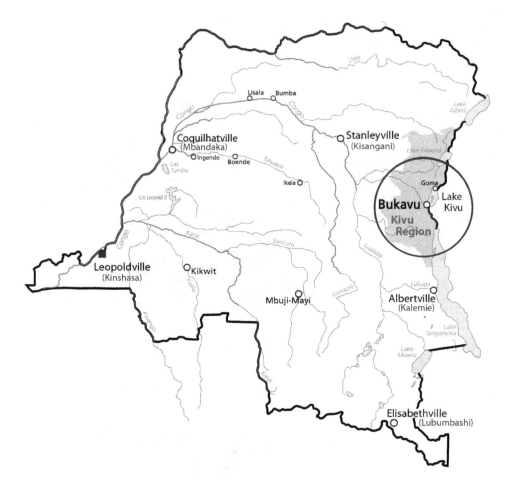

Democratic Republic of the Congo

Kivu Region of the Congo

Introduction

I N 1963 THE CONGO HAD BEEN an independent nation for three tumul-
tuous years. Ill-prepared for statehood, public order collapsed, virtually
as soon as independence was announced. The Army mutinied. Colonials fled. The Katanga copper-belt region in the southeast attempted
secession. The prime minister was assassinated. Rebellion broke out.

I came to the Congo as an American Foreign Service Officer, finishing
a break-in duty tour in Belgium. The Cuban missile crisis occurred while
I was in Brussels. The Cold War had Europeans, who were a few minutes
from the Soviet Nukes and a couple of weeks from the overwhelming Soviet
tank brigades. Rather than countering the Soviet tank buildup, NATO had
decided to deploy battlefield nukes to thwart them. Not an especially reas-
suring prospect to Europeans. The Soviets and NATO were jockeying for
position all over the world. Africa was in play. While I was in the Congo,
the American Embassy's primary mission was to thwart what appeared to
be very real Communist ambitions in Central Africa.

The Congo was quite a lively place. The Congolese were engaged in
a classic power struggle to determine who would rule in the absence of
colonial authority. Violence and mayhem were always possible.

However, the Congo did possess a kind of paradise, a province called the
Kivu in the far east of the country. The Kivu lay nestled among Rift Valley
lakes: Edward, Kivu and Tanganyika. The climate was benign, cool, and
healthful. The province boasted extraordinary beauty: mountains, lakes,
green and sparkling vegetation, and clear air through which to view it.
Bukavu, the capital, lay across five peninsulas stretching into Lake Kivu.

The Kivu had mostly escaped the chaos of the country's birth pangs
and the Cold War strivings it gave birth to. Kivu was peaceful, there
were plantations along the lake, people got along, and there was even an
hereditary African king, the Mwami of Kabare who lived atop the mountains behind the town.

I had the good fortune to be stationed twice in this glorious place.
I went there first in late 1963 having arrived in the Congo, a neophyte
United State Information Service officer who had just finished ten-months

training in Brussels, Belgium. I served in Bukavu until I was sent into the northwest, into the Equateur, to establish an American Cultural Center at Coquilhatville, a Congo River port. A year later, after being chased out of Coq by the Simba Rebellion, I was reassigned to Bukavu and finished my Congo tour there.

I loved the Kivu. Completely new to Africa when I arrived, all my perceptions alert, I embraced its experiences eagerly. This memoir contains six reminiscences from my first posting in the Kivu. The final three accounts relate experiences from my return there. The names of some people have been changed.

Three decades after these experiences, tribal massacres occurred in neighboring Rwanda. They sent refugees flooding into the Kivu, destroying what had made it seem a paradise.

As a result, these accounts chronicle a special time and way of life. They existed for only a few short years and now have vanished forever.

1
See-nay-ma

WHEN I ARRIVED IN THE CONGO, a US Information Service Foreign Service Officer who'd just completed a break-in tour in Brussels, Belgium, my assignment was Elisabethville. That was in the Katanga in the southeast. But in the capital, called Léopoldville then, I was told that eventually I would serve in the Equateur in the northwest. But first I would go to the Kivu on the country's eastern border. It was 1963. Things were a little confused in the Congo.

However, I was assured, "Bukavu is a place you'll love. Paul Wemboyendja will take care of you."

Wem-what? How did one pronounce that name? "We are damned lucky to have him working for us," said the officer briefing me. "It was a real coup to hire him away from the Kivu Information Ministry."

"In fact, we did not hire him away," corrected another embassy officer. "Not that operator. He sought us out the minute we arrived to set up a consulate. Asked if he could be of service. We made inquiries. Everybody said: 'Great contacts.' So we grabbed him."

Wemboyendja. Wem-boy-end-ja. Not difficult at all once you got used to it. In any case, I was immensely relieved that someone would show me the ropes in Bukavu.

The ill-prepared Congo had catapulted into national independence only three years before. It had suffered chaotic birth pangs. The army mutinied, refusing to obey Belgian officers. Colonials still resident in the country fled. The prime minister was assassinated. The copper-rich province of Katanga tried to secede. Its future was still being decided by parley and by arms.

The Kivu was quiet, but unrest had a way of traveling. The American Consulate in Bukavu, capital of Kivu Province, was keeping an eye on developments. The USIS operation, a cultural center and a films program, was designed to show Congolese that the Americans were friends. It demonstrated that friendship with goodies: books and pamphlets, displays and film showings.

Fred Hunter, Congo circa 1963.

In the absence of an American officer, Paul Wemboyendja was running USIS Bukavu. Despite his qualifications this was an extraordinary situation. Paul was a local employee; local employees did not supervise cultural centers. American officers did that.

Bukavu's USIS center stood on the town's main street. The consular offices were on a hill above the town half a mile away. The consul was in no physical position to know what went on at the center. Still he felt responsible for what happened there. Because of the Congo's reputation, USIS was having trouble finding an experienced officer to fill the post. The man slated for Bukavu had refused the assignment and resigned from the service.

That's where I fit in. In Brussels I completed Junior Officer Training, a ten-month tour, moving around the offices of a very different USIS operation. At an embassy in a European capital, home of the Common Market, USIS Brussels was directed by sophisticated attachés, a press counselor handling official statements, press conferences, and relations with journalists, and a cultural counselor setting up concerts, art shows, and various kinds of exhibitions. Almost nothing I learned in Brussels applied to the Congo. But because Belgians had colonized the country, it made a certain sense for me to be transferred there.

USIS' immediate need was for an officer to run the Bukavu cultural center. I was sent there on temporary duty.

Bukavu (Boo-KAH-voo) turned out to be a beautiful place. The town rode the backbone of Africa, nestled among mountains that receded line after line into the distance. It lay strung out atop five peninsulas, at the south end of Lake Kivu. In the colonial era Europeans lived in the town itself and in handsome homes on the peninsulas. The American consul, his wife, and two boys resided in one of these.

The Congolese lived in the *cités* of Bagira and Kadutu on the heights above the town. A looming presence on those heights was the Mwami of Kabare, a tribal potentate. His powers were real. But since Congolese were beginning to govern their own affairs in what might be called the modern style, those powers were also ambiguous.

Although Bukavu's beauty refreshed me, I was a bit uncertain what I was supposed to do. I hoped Paul Wemboyenda would prove friendly and a patient instructor of a young American new to Africa.

In fact, Paul was something of a rascal, a wheeler-dealer, and a suave ladies man. Fortunately, I enjoyed rascals, especially if they were amusing, friendly, and reasonably competent. Paul was. Before working for the Kivu Information Ministry he had served as a Lomani District delegate to the Congo's first constituent assembly. Prior to that he had helped local Europeans to escape across Lake Kivu after independence during what were called *les troubles.*

Paul had also been sufficiently influential (whatever that meant) to get beaten and tossed into prison when activists of the *Mouvement National Congolais* took control in the Kivu six months after independence. That was all in the past.

Paul was tallish, stocky, charming. He kept his hair clipped so close to his head that he always looked as if he were wearing a black pillbox hat. He had a roundish face, a ready sense of humor, and sparkling eyes. When you looked at him, you felt the good-hearted anticipation that fills the air when a comedian is performing.

The American Consulate in Bukavu, capital of Kivu Province, included a USIS operation, a cultural center and a films program, designed to show Congolese that Americans were friends.

Paul entered my office my first morning in Bukavu. I inquired, *"Tout va bien?"* ("Everything okay?")

He replied, *"Je vais bien"* ("I'm good"). That meant that he had heard, *"Tu vas bien?"* ("You okay?"). Oh-oh. "Tu" was the familiar form of "you" in French, a form colonials customarily used in addressing Congolese. I wanted to be sure he understood that I would not treat him as colonials had.

Having exchanged greetings, he announced, *"Je dois aller à Usumbura pour dire bonjour au pere de ma femme."* He had to go to Usumbura to "say hello" to his father-in-law. I was skeptical. Noticing that reaction, he added that his wife's mother had just passed on. He also needed time to attend her funeral. Hmmm.

Of course, Paul was testing me. Was I a stickler for discipline? It had grown sloppy in the months the center lacked an American officer. After the consul placed Paul temporarily in charge, he was frequently gone as he wanted to go now. He had been roaming around town in the USIS film truck, doing "contact work." In the evenings the truck was often seen parked outside nightclubs. There a man with a vehicle was always a magnet for women.

Yes, I was being tested. But why play martinet? I agreed that Paul could go to Usumbura, capital of the tiny nearby country of Burundi. If he liked to travel, so much the better. If I had any goal in Bukavu, it was to see some country.

When I told the consul that I authorized Paul's trip, he grumbled at me. He decoded what I'd been told. Step One: *"Dire bonjour."* "Saying hello" was apparently an African custom. Step Two: His wife's father. Paul's wife had left him, the consul explained. His trip was probably an attempt to resolve a dispute with her father. Or one of her fathers. Come again? The consul explained that Africans reckoned kinship differently than Americans did.

By African kinship reckoning the wife's father was not necessarily her biological parent. He might be any number of men senior to the biological father in the father's lineage. The same applied to the dead mother. Step Three: Why should he go? He was working at the center. Couldn't he *"dire bonjour"* on personal time? Probably, the consul said, he was behind on bridewealth payments.

He explained that Paul owed money all over town. His landlord had dropped by the consulate that very morning to complain that Paul had not paid his rent in five months. Did Americans not pay their employees? Another recent visitor was the father of an African girl (again that kinship ambiguity). He claimed that she was expecting Paul's child. Hmmm. What was to be done about this fellow with "great contacts"?

While he was out of town and away from the center, I worked with Dieudonné, the librarian, to regularize the operations of the library, the circulation and recovery of borrowed volumes and the proper reordering of them on the shelves. To a Congolese that ordering must have seemed a peculiarly American obsession. I also set up with Jean Rusenyagugu, the *planton* (janitor), a schedule for cleaning the building.

When Paul returned from Usumbura, without his wife, I began to keep better track of the after-hours use of the film truck. I accompanied Paul when he showed films in the *cités*.

One night we went to Bagira, high in the hills above Bukavu.

The film truck's appearance sent waves of excitement through the dusty streets. Children ran toward us, screaming "See-nay-ma! See-nay-ma!" and "Ay-tazz-oo-nee-dam-air-eeek!" (The legend *"Etats-Unis d'Amérique"* was painted on the film truck door.) Wild with anticipation, they danced in a frenzy, flinging their hips, and flailing their arms, clouds of dust rising about them. Paul leaned out of the window to greet them.

When we reached the *place*, the *cité* square, Paul started the phonograph blaring. The music was African, cha-cha-chas from his personal collection. The children danced more wildly. Dust motes flew up into the twilight. Young men joined the dancing. Paul quickly recruited them to help him to set up the film show.

Soon women abandoned their cook fires. With babies tied to the smalls of their backs, they approached the screen Paul had directed his acolytes to erect. He set up the projector beside the film truck. He chose the first film from the round canisters of them. He wound the film into the projector. Each operation heightened the excitement. When all was ready, he began the show with a *Charlot*, a Charlie Chaplin film. Slapstick in the balmy evening. Paul had his African audience in the palms of his hands. He held me there, too. Paul Wemboyendja was truly taking care of me in the Kivu.

We did film show after film show, always to eager crowds in Bagira or Kadutu, always beginning with a Charlot from Paul's personal collection. Next Paul showed USIS informational films. They gave our audiences glimpses of a world they could hardly comprehend, sometimes about developments that frankly bored them. But they stayed. While Paul rewound the films, our audience sang and danced. I did the twist, then in vogue in the States, to show that Americans also had moves.

Why did the audiences stay? Because Paul, that wonder-working impresario, had promised to end the evening with another Charlot.

When USIS Léo learned that we were showing Charlots, I received a stern instruction that they were not to be exhibited. USIS films were to inform, I was told, not to entertain. But Léopoldville was a long way off. Better to ignore the rebuke.

Sometimes after a film show Paul and I had dinner together. We ate at the Bodega, a quite splendid restaurant given the Congo's travails. It was located in the Hotel Royal Residence where Belgian royalty had stayed while visiting the town. We even had serious conversations.

One evening the subject was religion. Paul had two convictions about this matter. First, everyone should have a religion. Second, everyone should be free to choose the one he wanted. Pre-independence practices at the Bukavu cathedral offended him, he told me. He resented the fact that the heads of black children were shaved prior to baptism, but those of white children were not.

"*Le Bon Dieu* will punish these priests on Judgment Day," he said.

"Why's that?" I asked.

"They willfully refrain from marriage."

"And that's bad?" I myself had so far refrained from marriage.

"Marriage is the proper state of man," Paul said. "Each man has a duty to augment the world. *Le Bon Dieu* will punish these priests for their arrogance."

Paul Wemboyendja took care of me in Bukavu. In my turn I took care of him. I did this by taking possession of the film truck keys. I wanted him to keep his job. I drove the truck back to the consulate building where I lived on the second floor. If Paul intended to hit the nightclubs, as I'm sure he did, lighting them with his joy and laughter, known to young women as See-nay-ma, he would have to do it on foot.

2
Playing Toulouse

WHEN I ARRIVED IN BUKAVU, the consul told me, "You don't want to stay at the Royal Residence. It's a fine hotel, but you'll run through your per diem every day by the time you wake up. And then you've got meals. My wife and I would be happy to have you stay with us until the deputy arrives." The consulate's CIA officer, scheduled to appear in two weeks, was always referred to as "the consul's deputy." I would have to make room for him. "By then we'll have the apartment in the consulate building ready for you."

While I had expected to live in a hotel, I was quick to see that there were advantages to this arrangement. I had come to the Congo on a direct transfer from Brussels, Belgium. I had witnessed Foreign Service life in Old Europe. But I had no idea how it was lived in the underdeveloped world where posts might be small and remote with tiny staffs. The Bukavu consulate's American staff included only three of us: the consul, his radio man and me with "the deputy" soon to join us.

The Bukavu consul's residence was opulent. It sat atop a bluff overlooking Lake Kivu with islands spread out below. Blue mountains receded into the distance. A large, rather baronial home, it reminded me of a Swiss chalet.

Living *en famille* with the *Hillises* gave me a chance to see how a Foreign Service marriage worked in a small post. Carl Hillis was commanding, authoritative, often gruff, but with a ready sense of humor. His head was totally wrapped up in running the post.

Harriet Hillis provided the softness. I liked her very much. She treated me as if I were a cousin, which is to say that, although she did not know me, I belonged to the family.

A Foreign Service wife was not a State Department employee, but she had definite responsibilities. Her husband's advancement depended partly on her doing them well. Harriet ran the house and the servants. That was an involved task, given the amount of entertaining the Hillises did.

Entertaining was an important way for the consul to get to know the elite of the town and to ferret out what was going on in the Kivu. While

The Bukavu consul's residence was opulent. It sat atop a bluff overlooking Lake Kivu with islands spread out below. Blue mountains receded into the distance. A large, rather baronial home, it reminded me of a Swiss chalet.

I was living at the house there were all male lunches with African politicos, cocktails at 6:00 for wanderers passing through the town, dinners for expatriates, United Nations officials, and Belgians. Some colonials had never left, despite the downturns of independence; others had left and returned. I was invited to many of these functions. I considered this generous of the Hillises, but the consul expected me to do an effective representational job while being a guest.

Harriet also took care of the children. There were two boys, one ten, the other four. In addition, she acted as a kind of den mother for the consulate staff. Charley, the commo man, was having a romance with a young Belgian girl of good family, but of questionable reputation. Harriet wanted to be certain he handled that wisely.

She also took an interest in Mlle Moutarde, the consul's secretary. She was a sophisticated and attractive young Belgian who lived openly, unashamedly, with the young Volkswagen dealer. This was at a time when respectable Americans—and the Foreign Service is nothing if not respectable!—did not yet have live-in partners. Mademoiselle was nuts about the guy. He was largely indifferent to her, taking advantage of a good thing that had come his way.

I soon saw that, despite Harriet's warmth, there were tensions in the family. They became evident during the dinners I shared with the Hillises. Often they led me to excuse myself immediately afterwards and return to the cultural center to work or write letters.

The Hillises' two sons were as different as a pair of boys of the same parents could be. The older boy, Wilfrid, aged ten, was studious, shy, sensitive. When I met the family, Wilfrid was introduced as the resident chess master; I took it that he was well nigh unbeatable. Wilfrid, I learned, also read encyclopedias for pleasure. I was rather taken aback at this. What a weird kid! I glanced at his father for confirmation. The consul nodded his head. Wilfrid was not Will or Willy or Bill. He was his own kid, sensitive almost to the point of fragility.

But it was also true that Wilfrid was having a tough go of it. It could not have been easy, especially for a shy child, to be dragged around the world where it was necessary to start a new school every few years, make new friends, and do that in a foreign language. Somehow or other Wilfrid had broken a bone in his leg. He clumped around the house dragging a cast.

If the kid wanted to whimper now and then, I could certainly understand why. The trouble was that he whimpered all the time. In the morning he might appear at breakfast dissolving into tears simply because he'd been wakened from sleep.

"That's enough of that," Harriet would say.

The consul might add, "Okay, let's turn off the waterworks."

"I'm trying," Wilfrid would respond, a quaver in his voice. The quaver signaled a cracking of the dam, a flooding of the spillways. I would flee as quickly as I could and seek refuge at the office.

Toby, short for Tobias, was the exact opposite. At four, he was an extrovert, good with people, full of pep, and as charming a kid as I had seen in some time. One evening I witnessed a wonderfully tender byplay between the consul and Toby. Together they investigated the consul's wristwatch and compared it to a large clock in the hall.

Then the two looked at a figured tablecloth. *"Ou est la maison?"* the consul inquired in French, asking Toby to point out a figure in the cloth. Toby pointed out the house. The consul beamed. Toby was his kid. The two looked alike and had similar senses of humor. Toby could be a handful. I had a hunch the consul had been one at the same age.

A handful and also a rascal. Toby would shout (his father also shouted), stomp, and run his poor mother ragged. He also interrupted things constantly, particularly when guests were present. Toby knew how to use the tears, too, probably from watching Wilfrid. He needed discipline and would be warned, then carried physically from the room to give the grownups some peace.

I thought the whimpering had become habitual. Both boys used it as a way to negotiate with their parents. I thought it should have been brought under control years before. The fact that it hadn't meant that it might continue into adulthood.

It was also clear that the consul's career had priority. Perhaps when an FSO became a Principal Officer—Carl Hillis always pronounced those two words as if they bore capitals—work had to take priority. Harriet and the consul may not have wanted it that way, but they allowed the tradition of the service to set the rules.

Wilfrid concerned his father. Watching the child sometimes, the consul would shake his head. He once told me that he assumed Wilfrid would erect a shell around himself and take refuge in it. That could not have been a happy prospect. Even more distressing, now and then I saw a look on the consul's face that suggested that he did not really like his son.

A night or two before the CIA man arrived and I left, I thought to harmonize relations in the house. "Wilfrid," I said, "I wouldn't want to leave here before you'd beaten me at chess. Shall we have a match?"

Wilfrid looked surprised at this suggestion. While I assumed I was outmatched, he must have regarded me as three times his age and equipped with all the experience of adulthood.

"Go on," urged Harriet. "You enjoy chess matches."

Wilfrid clumped across the room on the leg with the cast. He fetched the chessboard and men. We set them up on a small table under a lamp and got ready to play.

"You better refresh my memory about how these guys move," I told him, studying the pieces: the king, queen, rook and knight, bishop and the pawns. It had been so long since I'd last played that it took me a few moments to keep them all straight.

Wilfrid explained the pieces. He had clearly read chess books as well as Britannicas. He began the match by moving forward a pawn. I responded by sending forth a pawn of my own. Our pawns did a minuet for several moves. Then the big guys marched out. We both studied the board, squinted our eyes, and stroked our chins. We made deliberate moves.

I had played no chess for quite a while. Still it was not hard to detect that the resident chess master's play was entirely defensive. Wilfrid did not play to win. He played to ward off defeat.

A shiver of alarm ran down my back. I had made two false assumptions: first, that Wilfrid would easily defeat me and, second, that victory would bolster his self-esteem. It would make him feel better about himself. But what if he lost? I suddenly glimpsed what I should have seen earlier. The whimpering, the encyclopedia reading, the taking refuge in a shell: these were all defensive strategies.

It was going to be very hard for Wilfrid to win this match. He would do that only if I started what I called Playing Toulouse.

I started trying, not obviously, to lose pieces. I succeeded for a time. But I didn't want to surrender so many that Wilfrid caught on and felt humiliated. When he saw what I was doing, he leaned over in his chair and complained, "Ohh! My stomach hurts!"

"Don't use that as excuse to stop the match," said Harriet.

I sat back from the board, hoping we could stop. As his mother came to watch us, Wilfrid found some courage. He made a move, one that practically sacrificed a knight to me. I could not ignore the opportunity and took the piece. Tears seeped into Wilfrid's eyes.

We continued to play. Harriet returned to her chair. Eventually it became clear that the defensive strategy could not prevail. Rather sheepishly, I won. In a quavering voice Wilfrid manfully declared, "I'm beat." He left our table and went to sit beside his mother, his eyes brimming with tears.

Harriet reached to put an arm about his shoulders. Suddenly he rose and gimped out of the room.

I glanced at Harriet, wanting to say how sorry I was that I had misread—But, face it, I had misread everything. Harriet sensed my chagrin. I realized that articulating it would only make things worse.

I left the house and walked around the neighborhood. How fragile we all are! That was what I thought. I trudged about for half an hour. When I returned to the house, everyone had gone to his room. I stayed alone in the living room, thinking how glad I would be to get into my own place.

For the rest of my tour in Bukavu, I felt pangs of guilt at having suggested that Wilfrid and I play a game of chess. The Hillises and I never spoke of it. They continued to be as generous to me as they always had been.

Through friends met in the Congo I kept tabs on the various postings of the man I've called Carl Hillis. He had a very distinguished Foreign Service career. He may have served as ambassador to Upper Volta (now called Burkina Faso), possibly as his next post after Bukavu. He certainly impressed people in the State Department. He must have picked up influential mentors. He later served as the American Ambassador to Poland and finished his career holding one of the positions of ambassadorial rank at the US Mission to the United Nations.

If Carl Hillis had a notably successful professional life, this was not the case for his sons. Neither of them married. Toby never finished college. He became infatuated with music-making, but lacked the talent and drive to succeed. As his father had foreseen, Wilfrid never learned to make friends. He spent his life inside the shell he built around himself.

3
The Future and The Past

A T A LUNCH AT THE CONSUL'S HOME, *Monsieur le Minstre de l'Interieur* Miruho talked so incessantly that hardly any of the rest of us had a chance. *Le Ministre* waved his arms. As his gesturing increased, so did the rush and tumble of his thoughts. When his momentum increased, his French grew less and less comprehensible.

The guests had been invited to honor the departing head of Bukavu's United Nations delegation, an Argentine named Carlos Gaviola. He and the consul had worked closely, fashioning a friendship. Beside the official consulate family, the guests were *le Ministre* Miruho, the thirty-four-year-old *Monsieur le Vice-President du Kivu Central, Monsieur* Rukara-tabare and Charles Morel, a Belgian neighbor who lived three houses down the road, had plantations in the Kivu, and relatives in Argentina.

The consul tried twice to interrupt *Monsieur le Ministre* Miruho, only to have Miruho increase the volume and speed of his remarks. The consul glanced at Gaviola and oscillated his eyebrows in resignation. Gaviola smiled, settled back in his chair, and reminded himself that tomorrow he would be gone.

Gaviola asked about Morel's wife and daughter. "Minou is growing up so fast," laughed Morel. "Sometimes I see a woman across a room at the *Cercle Sportif* and suppose she's thirty. Then she turns around and it's Minou." (I had seen her biking on our road and thought she might be thirteen.) Morel inquired about Gaviola's wife who had already returned to Buenos Aires. They spoke briefly about Argentina and, good host that he was, the consul tried to include his Congolese guests in this conversation. He explained to the two ministers where Argentina was. Neither had heard of it and showed no interest in it. They immediately redirected the talk to Kivu politics.

Gaviola, Morel, and the consul gave each other glances that tolerated the Africans. I myself thought it brave of the consul to attempt a social mixing of black and white, the *Assemblée Provinciale* and the *Cercle Sportif*, the future and the past.

The Congolese politicians were discussing practical politics. Not how to deliver benefits to their constituents, but how to get elected senator from Kivu next year. *"Mais, mon cher Vice-Président, comment dirai-je? Pas possible! Vous êtes trop jeune d'être senateur,"* intoned Miruho to Rukaratabare. ("My esteemed Vice-President, you are too young to become a senator.") Miruho hoped to nab that office himself.

"Mais, Monsieur le Ministre, je vous assure, je vais avoir trente-cinq ans avant les élections," Rukaratabare replied confidently. ("I assure you, I am going to be thirty-five before the elections.")

Ministre Miruho peppered each sentence with at least one *"comment dirai-je"* ("how shall I say") as if he were stumbling for his next words. But he was not stumbling into incomprehensibility; he had already achieved that. He always immediately followed that phrase with some word that required no pregnant introduction. It had been in his mouth all along, waiting to jump out.

The business of titles was very important to the politicians. The other guests observed with amusement as they flew around. Protocol was also important, for example, the order in which guests were served at the table.

Rukaratabare was especially sensitive about such things. The consul's servant seemed to think that Europeans, as whites were called, ranked higher than Congolese. He repeatedly served guests out of the order that Rukaratabare thought correct. He served *M. le Vice-Président* last, even after me. To show his irritation, Rukaratabare paused unduly before taking the serving utensils. In this way he underlined the servant's mistake.

When the luncheon was accomplished, the consul made appropriate remarks thanking Senor Gaviola for his significant contributions to the stability and development of the Kivu. Gaviola replied, saying how meaningful had been his too-short-a-stay in Bukavu. He also announced that he would this very afternoon make one last run to deliver food relief. His final destination was Shabunda, a small community about 350 kilometers west of Bukavu, deep in the jungle. He asked, "Would any of you like to come along?"

I jumped at the chance. As did *Monsieur le Ministre* Miruho. The consul gave his blessing to my going.

Sitting in metal bucket seats, we took off in a World War II cargo plane, painted white to indicate UN and ward off anti-aircraft fire from

At a lunch in the Consul's home . . . the Congolese politicians were discussing practical politics. Not how to deliver benefits to their constituents, but how to get elected senator from Kivu next year.

rebels in the hills to the south. Medicines, gasoline, and US-supplied powdered milk were strapped to the cargo floor. As the plane rose into haze, I looked directly below. Bukavu—and the Cultural Center!—passed beneath us. We quickly left the Rift Valley escarpment, let the altitude chill us, and flew west over the endless green of the Congo River basin.

Suddenly we saw that some of the green had been scraped away to make room for a town. We circled Shabunda twice to announce our approach. The arrival of the white plane and its cargo excited the entire community. Staring from the windows, I saw figures pointing to the sky, some racing toward the airstrip.

As we came in for the landing, the heat of the jungle offered its welcome. The plane settled onto the spongy grass runway cut out of thick vegetation in the very center of the town. As we disembarked, onlookers with silent, curious faces, all men or boys, greeted us from the edge of the runway, from behind a stake fence, from nearby trees. One tree must have held fifteen boys in its branches. They remained on their perches until we left an hour later.

Gaviola emerged from the plane and waved to the townspeople. He immediately began shaking hands with the local dignitaries. They were anxious to bask in the reflected glow of his presence. *Monsieur le Ministre* Miruho quickly moved beside him to wave and grasp out-thrust hands.

Local dignitaries proclaimed their thanks to the UN in French and feted Gaviola. He answered in French. *Monsieur le Ministre* took the microphone to express his thanks in Swahili and to do some politicking. He spoke about the future he could bring Shabunda as if the relief supplies we had brought were his doing.

At the edges of the crowd stood hordes of young men and boys. They crept forward to listen and observe with the same relentlessness that the jungle shows in reclaiming cleared land. A policeman tried to hush them. When they did not retreat, he picked stones off a gravel pathway. He hurled them. A cry arose. The boys dashed off with a high-hipped run that resembled stampeding gazelles.

I caught sight of a woman pushing her way toward us. The policeman backed away. She was white. Unique. And undeniably American, perhaps the daughter of the farm couple in Grant Wood's *"American Gothic."* A tallish, thin woman with a work-worn breastless figure. Her cheeks hung straight from the edges of her colorless eyes. Her mouth was thin, just a line across her face. A little stake fence of wrinkles ran above the bridge of her nose. Her hair dropped down from a knot that had come undone. Her dress hung on her as it might have hung on a hanger. Breathing heavily, she smelled as if she had run a long way.

She watched the speakers on the platform, then spotted me as a fellow countryman. Emboldened by this recognition, she approached me. "I'm Miss Helen Hoffman," she said. She smiled with a coyness decades out of practice. "An old maid missionary," she added. Her manner surprised me.

"I ran a mile to get here," she said, cocking her head to glance at me. Coquettishness may have been the only way she had ever known to talk with men of her own kind. "I came as soon as I saw the white plane circling." She looked down as if embarrassed. I saw that her bare feet in sandals were as splayed as the feet of a duck. "I've been here thirty-five years," she said.

"Really?" I could hardly believe that.

"Since 1928."

I nodded with encouragement.

"I'm with the Evangelical Bible Society of Pittsburgh, Pennsylvania," she said. "I'm particularly partial to spiritual work."

"Have you been back home in all that time?"

"This is my home."

"Of course. I meant—"

"Only twice back. Wouldn't leave at Independence. Even when it seemed like Armageddon. I had a house full of orphans. I preferred to die for them rather than leave."

"They must have been grateful to you."

She smiled shyly.

The relief supplies had been off-loaded. *Monsieur le Ministre* continued his politicking. We were called back to the plane.

"Before you go," Miss Hoffman said, "I must introduce you to two of my prizes." She ran to two men nearing middle age. They were standing nearby. She pulled them toward me to introduce them. One was the *chef du district*, the other a doctor. They shook my hand, treating her with affectionate respect, although she clearly struck them as odd, a sexless creature in a society that judged women by their procreative capacity. Still they willingly acted as evidence that she truly had accomplished great things in spiritual work.

When I shook her hand, saying goodbye, she once again murmured, "Just an old maid." She held my hand a moment, still Flapper Era girlish in the presence of a man like me. She was a jungle Rip Van Winkle. She had spent her life in the waking sleep of the deep bush, in that isolation chamber where every week was the same, where the daily routine of life and the annual passage of seasons never changed. It was as if she had been sleeping all those years in the eye of a storm that had never shaken her awake. Our dropping out of the sky was a mere stirring of her sleep.

"Goodbye," I said. "Nice to meet you." As I loosened my hand from hers, I hoped that she loved the Congolese, that her service had fulfilled her. I hoped that the donation of her life to the people of Shabunda had satisfied a longing for purpose.

Monsieur le Ministre was the last of our passengers to return to the plane. He grinned as if our stop in Shabunda had definitely advanced his senatorial campaign.

As we rose into the sky, I watched out the window. The last figure I saw was that of Miss Helen Hoffman, loping along the edge of the runway, waving.

4
Positively Curvaceous

At the end of their retirement trip to East Africa professors Tatianna Poulos and Charles Willson, academics from New York and a married couple, came to Bukavu to stick their toes into the troubled Congo. The trip was presented to them by students wishing to honor their contributions to sociology.

A dozen years before, Harriet Hillis, the consul's wife, had done graduate work with them. However, rather than finish her degree, she chose to marry the consul, a Foreign Service Officer about to leave for his first post overseas. The professors had not come pursuing research interests. They wanted merely to tell friends and colleagues that they had visited the turbulent Congo and receive the huzzahs their bravery would evoke.

As professors do, they kept in touch with promising students, even those who did not complete degrees. Knowing that Harriet was living in the eastern Congo, Dr Poulos wrote asking if they could "stop by" after visiting game parks in Kenya and Tanzania. Harriet replied that she and the consul would be delighted to have them "stop by."

She felt dismayed, she wrote, that she could not offer to lodge them at the consular residence, but fortunately, there was a rather decent hotel in Bukavu, the Royal Résidence. It had a good restaurant, the Bodega. Tatiana Poulos also noted that Dr Charlotte Keppel, a colleague of hers and Charles, was doing a year of research in Léopoldville. She might somehow get to Bukavu to see them while they passed through.

Drs Poulos and Willson arrived. The Hillises got them settled at the Royal Résidence, dined them at their home, and showed them around town, apologizing that there was not really much to see. The consul asked me to dine with them at the Bodega their second night in town. I looked forward to hosting them that evening. Americans with interesting backgrounds did not drop in on us every day.

The professors had a zest for travel and regaled me over dinner with places they had visited, thanks to the academic conferences they attended. East Africa was beyond the range of such meetings. They had chosen it for their retirement gift as unexplored territory.

Dr Poulos was short, trim, and probing, brightly interested in things. She had short, very black hair, wore glasses and despite an intellectual vivacity spoke slowly, ponderously, with frequent pauses that suggested she had lost her train of thought. Dr Willson observed his wife's search for words with an indulgent smile. Apparently a scholar of eminence, he would start to hold forth with a smile, perhaps with a witticism, or a striking turn of phrase. He then settled into a drone that left his dinner largely untouched while his wife and I had already finished ours.

The professors picked my brain about Bukavu and my short stay in Léo. I picked theirs about what they had seen in the East African game parks: elephants at Keekorok, rhinos in Ngorongoro, lions in trees at Lake Manyara, and zebras and wildebeest in Amboseli. I had been reading *The Serengeti Shall Not Die* and very much hoped somehow to wangle a trip to those places before I left the Kivu.

Their friend Charlotte Keppel negotiated an embassy flight to Stanleyville and would arrive in Bukavu early the next day. The consul asked me to fetch her at Kamembe airport, just across the border in Rwanda. Paul Wemboyendja was late arriving with the film truck; undoubtedly he had been out clubbing with it the night before and had found a companion. When I got to Kamembe, only ten minutes late, I was told that the plane had arrived early. Apparently Dr Keppel had hitched a ride into town.

When I reported this situation to the consul, annoyance flared in his face. "Was that damn Wemboyendja using the truck?"

I said that he was.

"You've got to take control of that guy. I know it isn't easy."

I assured him I would do better when I brought the three professors out to the consular residence that evening for a dinner with the Hillises.

But when I went to the hotel to pick up the trio about sunset, Dr Keppel was not there. Moreover, the Willsons had not yet seen her. I checked with the reception. Yes, Dr Keppel had checked into her room that morning, staying less than half an hour. Then she had gone out to look around the town.

I was not keen on letting the consul think I could do nothing right. The receptionist gave Dr Poulos a note in her key box. It said; "Tati, If I'm late for the dinner, go ahead without me. I'll get there."

"We can't just leave her," said Dr Poulos.

"Can you say, Asante sana? *" said Keppie. "Indeed we can," said Dr Poulos. "Do you think we did nothing but look at elephants and lions in East Africa?"*

"Would you want to call Harriet?" her husband wondered.

"What do you think?" she asked me.

I suggested we get into the film truck and drive the length of the town. Its main street stretched to the end of the longest peninsula. Perhaps Dr Keppel was window-shopping although that was an unlikely occupation for Bukavu. If we saw her, we could pick her up and take her to the Hillises.

I drove the professors slowly as far as the army camp at the end of the peninsula. Each professor scanned one side of the street. We did not see Dr Keppel. When we returned to the hotel, I suggested that we drive along the unchecked part of the main street. We did not find her there either. Since we were close to where the Hillises lived, I took them to the residence.

The professors embraced Harriet and shook the consul's hand. He did not seem unduly concerned. Dr Keppel would arrive on her own. But as soon as he had gotten us drinks, the professors started in on him.

"I'm terribly worried about Dr Keppel," Dr Poulos said.

"I don't think you need to be," the consul replied. "Shall we go out onto the terrace overlooking the lake?"

"Do you think something's happened to her?" asked Dr Willson.

"What could have happened?" said the consul with a smile. "This isn't Central Park."

"But it is the Congo," Dr Poulos observed. "Isn't it possible she's lost?"

"She's a white woman among Africans. She can't get lost."

I wondered if the consul believed this. Certainly mollifying the professors was the right response. We went out onto the terrace. Harriet passed hors d'oeuvres. The professors talked about their impressions of Africa as if the others of us were not living there.

Half an hour later, with the consul refreshing drinks and the cook holding dinner, Dr Poulos declared rather firmly that she was worried about Keppy.

"So am I," agreed Dr Willson. "You don't know Keppy. She's hopelessly punctual."

"She's been down in Léo for a while, hasn't she?" said Harriet. "One gets casual about time here."

"Perhaps," agreed Willson. "I noticed that very thing in Kenya." He beat his winter-bleached thumbs together and began to drone. His wife cut him off.

"The thing is," she said. "Keppy's not Congolese. I've never known her to be even five minutes late."

"Isn't the lake beautiful?" said the consul. Twilight was fading from the sky. Soon the lake would be cloaked in darkness.

"Once it's dark, how will she ever find us?" Dr Poulos asked.

The consul and his wife exchanged a glance. Harriet feared that her guests' concerns were going to derail her party. The consul gave a small shrug. "I'll call the hotel if you like," I said. But I saw that, in fact, he was not worried.

"Let's give her another few minutes," he suggested.

Dr Poulos settled back, knowing she mustn't insist. I could see that this was difficult for her; she seemed a woman whose academic position had made it customary for her to get what she wanted. "Keppy in Africa!" she said. "I can hardly imagine it."

Her husband chuckled in agreement. He described her to us: a deli-
cate, pale-skinned sociologist with hollow cheeks and long hair unfail-
ingly dressed in a bun. She walked across my mind in the gray tweed suit
and sensible shoes Willson mentioned as her characteristic attire. In my
mind I saw a parched, stereotypical maiden academic.

"How did she happen to come out here?" asked the consul.

"Did it in a fit of madness," Willson replied. "Utter madness!"

"It wasn't quite that," chided his wife. She looked at her watch and
tapped a finger against it. She explained that Professor Keppel had taken
a sabbatical year to conduct a study among Congolese women in Léopoldville.. "Do you know if she intends to finish out the year?" she asked.

The consul and Harriet looked blank. "I have no idea," said the
consul. In fact, none of us had met her. However, her finding her way
into Bukavu from Kamembe did suggest she took Africa in stride.

"She's certainly come a long way to see us!" Willson said. "Probably
lonely and homesick for shop talk." He began an explanation for us in his
instructor's mode. "You see, a maiden academic's social life is very bound
up in her professional relationships."

"Maybe she wants reassurance that her career won't be damaged if she
doesn't finish her study," broke in Dr Poulos. She was less patient with
her husband's style tonight than the night before when she had let him
rattle on. "No one in New York would blame her."

"Shall we go in?" suggested Harriet. She glanced at her husband, as if
to ask, "What now?' He gave her a smile.

As we returned to the living room, we heard a car drive up. A moment
later the lady entered. "Keppy!" exclaimed the professors.

"Darlings!" she said. "How nice to see you!" She embraced them and
kissed their cheeks in the French style. Harriet, the consul, and I introduced ourselves. Miss Keppel kissed our cheeks, too. Then she said to all
of us, "Don't you love this country!"

She was wearing sandals and a dress made of mammy cloth. It was
quite becoming: bold red and yellow flowers on a field of blue. She had
also cut her hair. A bandanna tied about it in the manner of Congolese
women matched the blue of her dress and accented the color of her eyes.
Her face had begun to tan. It appeared to have filled out as well.

"Keppy, it's really you!" said Charles Willson.

"Yes," she replied, leaning back comfortably, "really me. I'm sorry I'm so late."

The Willsons examined her so intently that she seemed a little uneasy. From their description I had expected someone's maiden aunt. But clearly that was not the person before us. She was not conventionally attractive. But as she talked, I saw that she had wonderful eyes and a ready smile. She seemed a woman likely to attract the notice of men.

Feeling more comfortable, she smiled. "I was walking around Bagira and lost track of time."

"Around Bagira?" asked Dr Poulos. "Isn't that where we drove the other day?"

"Yes," said the consul.

"You weren't there alone, I hope!"

"Of course I was!" she laughed. "It's not a bandits' hideout, you know, Tati. People live there."

"You're joking, Keppy!"

"Not at all. It's rather like where I live in Léo."

The Willsons stared.

"I loved it up there!" she said. "It vibrates with vitality: kids playing, trucks honking, women carrying pots on their heads and babies on their backs."

"Charlotte!" cried Dr Poulos. "Really?"

"Yes, really. I love to watch people gossiping in the market. And to hear their laughter. And all the while they're picking out red peppers and oranges, green plantains, and those stubby, sweet, yellow bananas, inspecting strawberries in woven baskets and live fish in bright enamel pans. I love the way their eyes shine when they laugh and the chocolate luster of their skin."

Charles Willson stared at her.

"I hiked down and started back along the lake. It was so beautiful! But it had gotten too late. I had to hitch a ride."

"You hitched a ride?"

"With a passing truck." She smiled. "The driver took me right to the hotel. The desk clerk brought me out here."

"I thought the housing in Bagira rather poor," commented Willson, rather formally.

"Yes, quite," Miss Keppel agreed. "It's even worse in Kadutu. The

The night was balmy. Below us lay the lake and the Bukavu peninsulas curling out into it. House lamps and cook fires showed through the darkness. Occasionally pairs of headlights shone from the Bagira road.

government is trying to improve it, though. Did you go past Bagira, up toward Kabare?"

"No, we found it too—"

"Oh, what you missed!" Miss Keppel exclaimed. "One of the best views in Africa! Really, this is a paradise here!"

At that moment the cook announced dinner. Miss Keppel rose and looked behind her out the window. "See what I mean!" She pointed to the lake. The last light was fading from it. "Look at that!"

But as we went to dinner the Willsons could only look at Dr Keppel.

Afterward we sat out on the screened porch. The night was balmy. Below us lay the lake and the Bukavu peninsulas curling out into it. House lamps and cook fires showed through the darkness. Occasionally pairs of headlights shone from the Bagira road. Miss Keppel gave a sigh of pure contentment.

"I think the Congo becomes you, Keppy," said Willson in a lightly teasing tone. "You've gained a bit of weight."

"You're positively curvaceous," commented his wife with a laugh. I felt certain the Willsons were wondering if their colleague had enjoyed any romances in Léopoldville. Before they saw her that had seemed beyond the realm of possibility; now it seemed likely.

"Nothing like palm oil to round a girl out," Dr Keppel said gaily in the darkness. "I've gotten new clothes, too. I threw all those gray suits away."

"Really?" said Charles Willson. "You plan to wear mammy cloth in New York?"

"Why not? It might be good for New York."

There followed a spate of shoptalk: about the distant city, their university and its sociology department, about new research, colleagues, and mutual friends. Tatiana Poulos mentioned several of Miss Keppel's students who wanted to be remembered. "You know," she said with a chuckle, "I think they'll hardly recognize you when you get back."

Dr Keppel smiled in the darkness.

"When are you returning anyway?"

"I'm not returning," she said.

"What!" The Willsons spoke together. Their mouths fell open.

"The study is more involved than I thought," she explained.

"You aren't returning till the end of your sabbatical then?"

"I'm not returning at all."

"Keppy!" blurted Dr Poulos.

"Your career is there!" exclaimed Willson.

They both stared at her.

"Keppy, dear, you've lost your perspective. New York is the center of things."

"Don't you miss it?"

"I do hunger for a concert now and then."

"Don't you miss *us*?"

"Of course," she said with real warmth in her voice. "I think of you often"—teasing them gently—"slogging about in snow under gray skies or tramping sidewalks in wan sunlight with newspapers blowing about your feet."

After a moment she said more seriously, "And I've thought of myself: thin, alone, walking for winter exercise down endless streets, wearing old maid's shoes and gray tweeds. Hungering for color without knowing it."

"I believe you really *want* to stay here, Keppy."

"Yes, I do, Tati," she said. "I'm happy here. I'm rounded and tan. I wear mammy cloth. I work with people, not statistics. Now and then I'm conscious of men watching me. I've found color. I live in it and it's lovely." She smiled like a late-blooming flower that had found its time.

Later, saying goodbye, the Willsons stood apart, their thin, white arms folded across their chests. Once again they waited for Dr Keppel. She was in the kitchen, thanking the cook.

"I can't believe it," whispered Willson to his wife.

"Extraordinary, isn't it!"

"Keppy's going to be downright beautiful if she doesn't watch out!"

As I drove them back to the hotel in the film truck, Willson asked, "What in the world were you doing so long in the kitchen, Keppy? You weren't getting the recipe, were you?"

"I was thanking the cook for the dinner. I tried my kitchen Lingala on him. He grinned at me. So I switched to my three or four words of Swahili. Can you say, *Asante sana*?"

"Indeed we can," said Dr Poulos. "Do you think we did nothing but look at elephants and lions in East Africa?"

The Prince Sees the Mwami

A S THE USIS FILM TRUCK LEFT BUKAVU and the peninsulas stretching into Lake Kivu, I felt pleased with the prospect of the day. Night rain had washed the haze from the air. The morning was clear and sunny. As we climbed toward the *chefferie* of Kabare, I was happy, wedged between two companions on the truck's torn seat. Paul Wemboyendja was driving. Next to the window sat Mark Stern, a correspondent for America's premier newspaper.

As we left the lake shore and moved up into the hills, I appraised Mark. We were about the same age, not yet thirty. Mark might even be younger. But he carried himself like a prince. That came with the position. Hmm. Was I jealous of Mark? Maybe. Why not? Great job, great perks. Everyone deferred to him, hung on his words. They suggested sources, checked his coverage to see if he'd used their tips. Moreover, the guy had a bedmate in Léopoldville, a Belgian girl I had dated in my brief time down there. The bedmate: maybe she too came with the position. Mark really was like royalty, visiting the far reaches of America's empire.

The consul had met his plane, briefed him, visited his hotel, arranged dinners for him, taken charge of his weekend activities, even kept him informed of cable traffic. The consul told me, "Any help you can give this reporter or his paper, you be damn sure you give it."

"This visit should be fascinating," I observed.

Mark peered out the window at the shimmer of the lake, at the mountains receding in blue hues all the way to the Ruwenzoris. He turned to Paul. *"Quel jour, eh?"*

"Ah, oui, Monsieur!" said Paul.

On the road women trudged down from the hills, balancing baskets of strawberries on the straight columns formed by their backs, necks, heads. I surveyed the patterns of the cloths tied about them. Mark studied the huts of the villagers. Was he wondering how to describe them?

At Mark's request, we were on our way to visit the reclusive Mwami of Kabare. The consul had set up the interview. He'd sent a messenger to the office of the *chefferie*, requesting that the Mwami show Mark Stern the hospitality of the region. He had further specified the hour, suggesting that the Mwami offer this hospitality at 10:00 the following morning. Nice for a journalist to have all that help, I thought. I wondered if Mark loved Africa, as I was beginning to, or merely covered it.

Mark probably wondered how his editors would play the story. The fight for space in the paper was rugged like the fight for space in the jungle. Mme Nhu, the Vietnamese dragon lady, was at this moment in New York, demanding coverage. MacMillan had just resigned in Britain. The Congo story was also being covered from the UN. Unless the Mwami said startling things, the piece might get killed. Bastards. Or they'd bury it on page 20. Next to the Gimbel's ads.

It was some story, I thought. An interview with an African king, demigod to some, autocrat to others. Mark might have already worked out his lead: "Being received by the Mwami of Kabare, absolute ruler of a quarter million tribesmen here, is like stepping four hundred years back into 1563." I had heard him tell the consul that he might portray the Mwami as a traditionalist rogue, a charming anachronism. He might sprinkle gems of Mwami wisdom throughout the piece. He and the consul had laughed about that.

As we climbed toward Kabare, I noticed the green fluttering of banana leaves, the burnt umber of the earth. As Paul drove, he waved to the Kabare women we passed. They stopped to watch the van, their whole bodies turning. Recognizing it, they called "See-nay-ma! See-nay-ma!"

They knew Paul; he worked for the white men; he controlled an entire roomful of their equipment and gave film shows in the communes. Paul waved in a gesture of noblesse oblige. He did not admire muscular work-hardened bodies or bovine stares. The women he preferred were rounded and laughing. He waved because women were women.

"Paul, mon ami," Mark said. "During this interview, there may be stuff I don't get. You'll walk me through it afterwards, okay?"

"Bien sur, Monsieur," Paul said, grinning. "Bien entendu."

Pleased with himself, he tooted the horn at an old man hobbling across the road. The consul and I were treating this famous journalist from New York with such deference that Paul wanted to render whatever service he could. Perhaps the man needed an assistant. Or a representative in the Kivu. Perhaps Paul should inquire discreetly if he needed a woman. What man did not need a woman?

"This Mwami's some potentate," Mark remarked to me. "Colonial authorities exiled him twice. First time for twenty-three years. Set up a puppet in his place. You realize that?" I recognized the consul's briefing and nodded. "Then when he returned, he had the puppet Mwami and two retainers beheaded. Right?"

I shrugged. The consul relished stories that made him seem to be holding the line against barbarism. During the summer he had cabled Washington to report that the Mwami had forbidden Kabare women to carry wood into Bukavu, cutting off a commodity important to the town. According to the consul, the Mwami had confiscated trucks from coffee and tea plantations.

Occasionally the Mwami boasted that he would descend into Bukavu with hundreds of warriors to force his claim against Europeans who had taken Kabare land without ever compensating him for it. He would punish Kivu politicians for presuming to rule in his stead.

"The Mwami ordered two tribesmen to be buried alive last week," Mark said. "You hear about that?"

I watched the road. I was thinking that "potentate" and "tribesmen" were journalist's words. Had I ever seen those words used outside news reports?

When I did not reply, Mark examined me. Probably he thought I had not been in Africa long enough to respond as Africans did, inspecting questions from every vantage before committing themselves. So why was I studying my answer? I might seem bright enough. But at the consul's dinner for him Mark would have noticed that I neither drank nor smoked. Probably I was not getting much either. I had seen some of the world, but would not take a bite of it. Mark might wonder: Why was that? I wondered myself.

Mark asked again, "You hear about those guys?"

"Lot of stories fly around," I said.

"You don't think they're true?"

"What is truth? Didn't somebody ask that?"

"Is it factual?" Mark asked, a little pissed. He was trying to put together a story.

"I guess it's factual," I said. "In Africa it's *why* that's so puzzling."

Mark shook his head. He probably thought: What a jerk!

I thought: As if facts alone meant anything. But I did not say it. Why say it? Why cast doubts on the consul's careful briefing?

"Does this sound factual?" Mark asked. "Last week an excited tribesman rushed to police officials here to report that the Mwami of Kabare had ordered villagers to bury two men alive. The officials raced up to Kabare. They found two men buried up to their necks and managed to rescue them."

I thought: Maybe that's the lead he's working on.

I said. "Sometimes I wonder if the Mwami and his counselors don't get bored up in the hills. So they say, 'Hey, let's see how long it takes them today.' They find someone who's been questioning the Mwami's authority and they give both him and the government of Kivu Central a scare."

Mark shrugged.

"Ought to be a great story," I assured him. "Your readers'll get some idea of what's at stake in bringing this country into the modern world." I said this because I supposed it was what the consul would want me to say. I added, "I can see guys over coffee telling their wives, 'Hey, honey, you better read this.'"

Mark nodded. The USIS man was not supposed to fight him and, good, he wasn't going to. A tight, satisfied smile appeared on Mark's mouth. Suddenly he craned his neck at the sight of a child picking lice from the braided hair of a woman. He took a pad from his jacket and made a note.

The film truck climbed past Bagira, one of the communes colonial authorities had built to house workers lured away from Kabare villages. It left the paved road, ascending toward low-hanging overcast on the mountain tops. The air was cool here. Paul held film shows on the Bagira soccer field. He saluted it by honking the horn. Children receiving lessons in a roadside school stood at the sight of the truck. Paul leaned from the driver's window to wave. Children broke from their class. They ran beside the truck yelling, "See-nay-ma! See-nay-ma! Ay-tazz-oo-nee-dam-air-eeek!"

Paul tooted the horn, delighted at celebrity-hood. I watched him mildly distressed. The consul had seen the film truck parked outside nightclubs and was concerned about appearances. I understood that in Bukavu the truck was an aphrodisiac. It excited desire in the many young Congolese women who had never ridden in a vehicle of any kind. They would gladly offer Paul access to their bodies for a chance to ride in the truck. I worried that Paul was exploiting their generosity and possibly damaging our reputation.

Moreover, the previous week Paul had sought an advance of 25,000 francs. When I asked the consul's advice, he said, "Don't give that guy a penny! He owes me 10,000 francs!"

Paul pulled himself back inside the van. *"Tout le monde m'aime,"* he told us. ("Everybody loves me.") In the rear view mirror he watched children chasing him. *"Tout le monde m'appelle Cinéma!"*

I nodded and wondered yet again: What do I do about this guy?

Outside the village of Kabare, oil drums blocked the road. A young guard wearing a brown beret with "Kabare" sewn on it in white thread sat on a stool. In his hands he played a *likembe*, a "thumb piano," plucking its metal strips fastened to a sound box. Reaching the roadblock, the truck stopped. Eventually the guard moved to the truck. He peered at its passengers. Paul gestured to Mark and explained in Swahili that the Mwami was awaiting this important guest.

The guard nodded and pushed two oil drums out of the road.

"The Mwami has his own police?" Mark asked Paul.

"Bien entendu, Monsieur," Paul replied. "And his own tax-collectors. The government of Kivu Province, it's a joke up here."

Mark nodded and made half a page of notes in his pad.

The offices of the Kabare *chefferie* were open, but deserted. Mark's mouth tightened. He walked through the building, muttering: "Shit! Your consul better not have fucked this up!" He was scheduled to catch a four o'clock plane to Usumbura; there he would file his story. He shot me a glance that said, "I thought you guys set this up."

I thought: "Easy, Pulitzer. Where do you think you are?"

An old man appeared. He wore frayed shorts, a threadbare overcoat and a black policeman's cap green with age. No, the Mwami was not coming to the *chefferie* offices, he told Paul in Swahili. No, there was no appointment. No, the Mwami did not accept to receive American journalists.

I thought: "Easy." The old man might not even know what a journalist was. The muscles around Mark Stern's mouth pulled tighter. Yes, the old man agreed, he would conduct the three visitors to the Mwami's *palais*.

The "palace" proved to be a complex of buildings, dominated by a large house a European planter had abandoned three years earlier when the Congo acceded to independence. The old man departed to announce our arrival to the Mwami.

In a small meadow fenced with chest-high bushes two horses grazed. "The guy keeps horses?" Mark surveyed the surroundings and made notes in his pad.

Glancing around, I thought how heady it must be to live in mountains that scraped the clouds. The gods were supposed to live here. Well, I mused, why not here? They had to live somewhere.

This may have happened out of our sight:

The Mwami sat on the porch of his palace in pajamas and slippers. He had finished the mid-morning ritual of receiving the tribal notables and clan heads. He watched the horses, thinking about a dispute between two clans that he must adjudicate.

A young man who attended him hurried onto the porch. He bowed low and waited to be recognized. The Mwami said, "Speak." The young man reported that two white men were on the lawn, accompanied by an African who was not one of the people. The Mwami nodded.

The young man stood, apparently desiring to speak again, but nervous. It tired the Mwami to see a young man in his service who became agitated at the mere approach of white men. Was he not, after all, the Mwami of Kabare, chief of all the lands hereabouts? And were the white men not mere supplicants? The Mwami flicked his hand tiredly. The young retainer bowed low and withdrew. The Mwami looked back at the horses. The whites could wait.

Paul watched the Mwami's horses frolic in the meadow, cantering in large circles. Presumably to show the prince from New York that he was a man of the world, he enthused, *"Ah, j'aime les chevaux."*

Mark ignored him. I smiled to myself. As if he rode.

When the old man did not reappear, the three of us drifted toward the Mwami's house. We came upon a group of ancients clustered on the steps of a side porch. Many of these men smoked pipes and wore what I thought of as goat beards, straggly collections of tightly coiled chin hair, some of the hairs whitening. Two of the men protected their old heads with monkey-skin caps. Dressed in patched jackets and shorts, in baggy, uncreased trousers turning purple with age, they beheld us newcomers suspiciously. *"Les notables,"* Paul whispered. "Tribal elders come every morning to greet the Mwami."

Mark nodded. He watched the old men as intently as they watched him.

Because two of us were white men, the notables stood and stepped forward. They presented themselves with caution and a certain rigidity. They bowed slightly, folding forward stiffly, and offered their hands. We shook them, bowing slightly with deference, then stepped back.

While the ancients examined us, Paul explained in Swahili that Mark Stern, gesturing to him, was a very important visitor whom the Mwami had agreed to receive. The ancients gazed at Mark out of eyes so old that streaks of brown discolored them. They said nothing.

Paul sensed difficulties. They need not be conveyed to the Americans. The Mwami had forgotten the meeting. Or had never been told. The Americans must not know. Paul saw the notables glancing toward the front of the *palais*. Still praising Mark and his paper, Paul looked in that direction. He saw the figure in the chair. He recognized and broke toward it, exclaiming, *"Bonjour, Mwami!"*

Mark hurried forward. I grabbed his arm, held him back. Mark shot me a glare of fury. "Slow down," I whispered. "That's a king."

"Take your fucking hand off me," Mark muttered.

But I did not release my grip until Mark stood respectfully, waiting for the Mwami to signal to him.

The Mwami may have done and thought this:

He leaned his head back in the chair. His eyes started to close. Suddenly behind him footsteps sounded. Before he could look around, he saw a grinning face bending toward him. *"Bonjour, Mwami,"* the face said.

The Mwami sat up, thought, "Who is this? How dare he approach without being announced?" Then he recognized the pushy fellow his people called *"Cinéma,"* the white man's toady who considered himself a great personage because he drove the white man's truck and wore his clothes and spoke his language. *Cinéma* of eager grins, a pudgy frame, and a smooth, fast tongue. He had dark skin, almost black, and was not one of the people. The Mwami recalled hearing that he came from the grasslands on the far side of the mountains. He might be a dignitary in Bukavu, but in Kabare he was a nuisance, an upstart.

Cinéma stepped back. He put his feet together and bowed, an overdue gesture of respect for the Mwami's power, for his being.

Cinéma did not bow low, the Mwami noticed. A feigner of obsequiousness to the white man, he supposed a Mwami would not know true respect. He dared to stand in a Mwami's presence unannounced. As if a Mwami would not distinguish between true respect owed a man of power and the feigned deference shown to white men.

"I bring an American who desires to talk with the Mwami," this *Cinéma* said. He talked on, but the Mwami stopped listening, feeling cold now in his pajamas and old in the presence of this black-skinned outsider from the grasslands who knew no decorum.

The Mwami looked off toward the clouds that shrouded the trees. What kind of white men were "Amay Ricans," he wondered. Belgians, he knew and hated. And the new rulers: toad-eaters, jackals in men's skins, former postal clerks, to whom the people were said to have given power by dropping papers into a box. He was beginning to know them. But Amay Ricans, the Mwami did not know. He had heard that they came to steal the land. He must beware of them.

"The consul sent a letter, Mwami. The journalist wishes to ask you questions—"

The Mwami looked up sharply. *Cinéma* stopped his smooth tongue. Ask questions? Truly, this *Cinéma* knew no decorum. Visitors entreated. Visitors begged humbly. Or sought the Mwami's patronage. But questions? No! If there were questions, it was the Mwami who asked.

The upstart began speaking again, but the Mwami did not listen. He stood. Attendants appeared from inside the palace. The white men's menial burst into smiles, thinking his request had been granted. "An important man, you say?" the Mwami asked. He spoke Swahili because he would not use the white men's words.

"Very important, Mwami." The toady grinned like a hyena when it smells carrion. He extended an arm, gesturing toward the porch where his masters waited.

"I cannot receive an important white man dressed as I am now dressed," the Mwami said. "You see how I am dressed."

"He will be honored to see you just as you are, Mwami," this *Cinéma* said. Finally he bowed low.

"Because he is important," said the Mwami, "it is proper for me to show respect for that importance. Just as a Mwami might expect to receive the respect rightly accorded a Mwami."

The hyena grin faded from the fawner's face.

"Tell him that the Mwami is not yet ready to receive important visitors. Have him wait."

As the Mwami moved toward the house, one of his young men opened the door. The Mwami entered and did not look back.

"Oooo la la!" Paul must have thought. "With this Mwami there are always difficulties. But the Americans must not know." He put a grin onto his face and stepped lightly across the grass. *"Bonnes nouvelles, Messieurs,"* he announced. "The Mwami is honored that you're here. He wants to receive you in a way that befits the occasion!"

Mark was accustomed to this sort of reception and felt encouraged. Things were working out. He opened his notebook to the question list. A couple of controversial ones. Good!

I was relieved that Paul had come through. They were right in Léo. The guy did seem to know everyone. I wondered what a "potentate" made of the Western ceremony of the press interview.

A young man who said he was the Mwami's secretary appeared from inside the house. He carried himself with a dignity that merited attention from Mark. Was this the Kabare heir the consul had mentioned, the young man of promise the Mwami had adopted as his son?

The secretary invited the visitors to enter the house. He escorted them onto a small, enclosed porch where two other men awaited the Mwami. He showed Mark and me to heavily upholstered chairs drawn up on opposite sides of a low table. Paul stood against a wall.

Minutes passed. No one spoke. Paul took a seat.

One of the waiting Africans turned out to be a *chefferie* tax collector. Mark zeroed in on him. He had heard, Mark said, that the Mwami collected taxes in cattle that the government had not authorized. Was this true?

The tax collector glanced at the secretary. The secretary's expression did not change. The tax collector denied that the Mwami collected unauthorized taxes. He had heard, Mark said, that the Mwami set taxes according to his whim. Was this true? No, it was not true, said the tax collector. If farmers did not pay the taxes demanded, Mark asked, was it not true that the Mwami's police threw them off their land? The collector denied that this was true.

The secretary spoke to the tax collector. Mark and I glanced at Paul. He shook his head perplexedly, indicating that he could not follow what was being said. The secretary departed. For some moments no one spoke.

Mark jotted notes in his pad. After a time, the tax collector explained that the farmers did not own the land they farmed. The Mwami owned it, for the people. The farmers used it at the Mwami's pleasure. Mark nodded and made more notes.

Several notables entered. They bowed stiffly and extended their hands. I rose to shake them. I resumed my seat, watched Mark making notes. "The guy's never left New York!" I thought. Here we were in a place so remote that whites had not settled it until after the First World War. We were waiting for an audience with a Mwami who beheaded people when he felt like it or had them buried alive.

Was it not obvious to Mark that he and the Mwami lived by different codes? Mark Stern's code gave Mark Stern the right, nay the obligation, to grill people he interviewed. He could interrogate the Mayor of New York, who accepted his code, on the way taxes were collected. But the Mwami of Kabare?

I hoped the Mwami felt generous this morning. Then he might just let Mark and Paul and me walk out of Kabare alive.

Long minutes passed.

A young African joined the group. "You are Americans?" he asked in English. "I learned English in Kenya," he explained. Then he added, "I have come to petition the Mwami for money. To continue my studies. It would be well, don't you think, for the Mwami to have someone in his household who speaks English?"

"Tell me," Mark said, watching him. "The Mwami's secretary. He was here a few minutes ago. Is he the Mwami's heir?"

The petitioner's face went blank. He studied the question.

I thought: Mark must know what he's doing. But I myself would not have phrased the question so directly.

At last the petitioner asked, "Air?" He waved his hand through the air. "So many words the same in English."

"That's true," said Mark. He made more notes in his pad.

This may have happened out of our sight:

The Mwami smoked a pipe while waiting for his attendants to lay out his clothes. He remembered the first white man he had ever seen.

He was very young then, the adopted son and presumed heir of the Mwami who preceded him. That Mwami had received in a night vision a warning from the ancestors that beings from the dead would come to Kabare. Late that day warriors raced into his court to tell of a being with white flesh and hair the color of sunset. The being had entered Kabare and was building a camp where the fingers of land extended into the Water of the Ancestors. Many women had left off tilling to watch him.

In the Mwami's court the vision and the warriors' report caused profound apprehension. A being with flesh of a hue seen only on the dead? What did this portend for Kabare? The young man who would become Mwami had returned with the warriors to watch.

The being with white flesh bartered with beads and mirrors for food and drink. He ate with his mouth. He squatted to defecate and stood to make water. When the being washed in a stream, his whiteness stayed. So this whiteness was not made by ashes rubbed on his skin. All of his flesh was pink-white and except for its color his body was in every way like the bodies of Kabare men. The being came from a people who did not circumcise. The Mwami reported all of these observations to his predecessor.

The being stayed at his camp many days, hunting gazelles with a stick that spat metal and roasting their flesh. He picked fruit without regard to who had the usufruct (the legal right to use someone else's property) of the trees. He plundered materials and constructed a shelter in a form different from any ever seen in Kabare. The being enticed a maiden into his shelter and lay with her. Although he mounted her in a manner little known in Kabare, the being seemed to have the same desire for a maiden's body that warriors felt. Warriors, however, controlled these desires. The white being did not.

The notables of Kabare held counsel with the Mwami. Some said that the being—since he ate, slept, relieved his body of waste and desired maidens just as the men of Kabare did—was a man like other men. As lions and leopards were much the same except for the markings of their hides and some of their habits, so this white being was a man not unlike themselves.

The Mwami of that day concluded otherwise. He proclaimed that the being was a spirit of the dead. The present Mwami had always accepted that conclusion.

Mark placed an X at the end of a sentence. He looked over what he had written.

"That your story?" I asked.

Mark looked at his watch. "It's 11:47."

"Head of the U.N. team in Bukavu waited two hours to see the

Mwami," I said. "And he was offering more than his name in the paper."
I grinned. Mark was not amused. "We've only been here—What?"

"One hundred and ten minutes," Mark said. "You don't wear a watch?"

"Gave it up. When in Rome."

Minutes evaporated like the fog that had lifted outside.

The secretary who claimed to speak little French appeared. *"Entrez,
Messieurs, s'il vous plaît,"* he offered, inviting us into a parlor. For a *"palais"*
the room struck me as small. Three heavy couches of post-Victorian design
diminished its size. An archway stood across from us. Lengths of thin,
un-hemmed material curtained off the room beyond. Mark shot me a
look. "I'm supposed to file this afternoon," he said. "This gonna happen?"

"This is not a deadline culture," I remarked.

Mark raised an irritated eyebrow.

We heard someone moving behind the curtains. The Mwami? I saw
shoes visible below the pink and beige material. I caught Mark's eye and
nodded toward the shoes. Mark noticed them, but said nothing. When
the shoes disappeared, Mark said, *"Paul, mon ami. Ça marchera?"* ("This
gonna happen?")

"Oui, ça marche, Monsieur," Paul told him. *"Bien sur! Le Mwami
comprend que votre journal est tres important!"* ("Oh, sure. The Mwami
understands that your paper is very important.")

Mark nodded. The muscles of his mouth grew tight once more.

I watched the lengths of material. The shoes reappeared behind them.

This may have happened beyond our sight:

As they prepared the Mwami to hear a dispute among the clans, his
attendants set out the hat of colobus monkey skin that he would wear.
They took from its box the leopard skin they would drape over his shoulders. Impatient, the Mwami returned to the room where from behind
the closed curtains he observed the white men. He watched his notables detain the men as he had directed them to do. He studied the man
writing in the notepad. This business of asking questions, he thought.
It was a game of mischief and trickery the white men played. Why they
played it, he did not understand.

Long ago it had been possible to humor white men who asked questions. Such men would be brought into court. While the Mwami stood
in the rear, watching the visitors, a notable would greet the men. He
would listen to their questions. Perhaps he would offer replies. While this

happened, the Mwami would examine them.

But this was no longer possible, for *Cinéma*, the white men's toady, knew who the Mwami was. Now a Mwami must study visitors by watching behind a curtain. The Mwami returned to his dressing room. He told his attendants to offer the white men beer.

Mark wrote in his notebook. A servant arrived with two glasses of beer. He set one before Mark, the other before me. We exchanged a glance. Eight men, two beers? We would not drink if the others were not served. We ignored the beers.

Paul watched them thirstily. I saw that the shoes that kept watch behind the curtains had returned. I signaled Mark.

He nodded. So the Mwami was watching us. Mark probably felt an almost undeniable urge to rush the curtains, grab the Mwami, and say, *"Votre excellence, je voudrais vous poser quelques questions."* ("Excellency, I would like to ask you some questions.") What would the Mwami do? The fact that Mark did not know kept him sitting at the table.

This may have happened out of our sight:

The Mwami watched the white man with the notepad. So he came to ask questions about taxes! What insolence! Who sent him? What did he really want?

The Mwami perceived behind the open, smiling face the self-importance that most white men possessed. If he permitted the man to enter his presence, he would ask if the Mwami buried people alive. Or if he beheaded them. The whites were always curious about death. Because they were beings from the dead.

A Mwami embodied his people. Did the white man not know this? A Mwami sought to rule by consensus. Did the notables not greet him every morning to inform him of problems demanding his attention? In this way a Mwami strengthened the people.

But if some man challenged a Mwami outside the established system, if he blocked consensus, if he sought to excite the people to rebellion and imperil unity. . . Well, he must be warned. If he persisted, he must be punished. Sometimes it was enough to bury such a man up to his head. After a day or two he saw that the Mwami's authority must be maintained.

But if he continued to think that his own will was more important than the people's unity, then he was beheaded. Because a Mwami's power

. . . the islands, the mountains, the clouds were not realities at all. They were dreams, yearnings that nature had given blue shapes. They were longings set across an uncrossable stretch of dark and silvered water.

wasted away if he did not use it. Because the people must know that survival depended on submission to the Mwami. The Mwami alone protected their future.

Watching the white men, the Mwami understood that if he granted them an audience he would jeopardize the health of his people. When these white men left, they would do their small something, whatever it was, to hasten the death of Kabare.

The Mwami stepped back from the curtains and called for his car.

I studied the room's adornments: the elephant tusk, the small Kivu drums, the animal horn carved to resemble a fish, the two beers going flat.

"I wouldn't wait this long to interview President Kennedy." Mark said.

"You can wait," I told him. "Or you can blow it."

Mark whimpered, "I want my Mwami!"

I bit my tongue so as not to laugh. The notables regarded us curiously.

"Mwark mwants his Mwami."

I stared at the floor, trying not to laugh.

"Mwaiting for Mwami mwakes Mwark mweary."

Suddenly the pink and beige curtains parted. Mark stood, ready to smile, ready to bow, or offer his hand. A notable with a cane hobbled into the room. He announced, *"Le Mwami est parti."*

Gone? Mark looked at me, at Paul. Gone? We were standing now, perplexed looks on our faces. Gone? How? We heard a motor. We rushed onto the porch.

A black Mercedes was parked outside the house, its engine idling. The Mwami sat inside it. He wore a leopard pelt over his shoulders and a hat of a colobus monkey skin. As soon as he saw the two of us, he signaled the driver. The car sped down the driveway and out of sight.

Mark was furious. He turned to complain. But the notables had disappeared. The secretary who spoke no French was still on the porch. "Does the Mwami always act this way?" Mark asked the secretary curtly in French.

"Easy, Pulitzer," I soothed.

"I'm not Foreign Service," Mark replied. "Fuck it! Fuck them!" He swore in French at the secretary who spoke no French.

"Don't mess it up for us," I said.

Paul appeared, wiping his hand across his mouth. He had dispatched the beers. Mark swore at him. The secretary disappeared. "I have a certain tolerance for African custom," Mark said, "but this is going too far." He started toward the house.

"Don't get moralistic," I advised. "That won't help."

"Fuck you!" Mark said. "Piss-ass USIS man. Fuck you!"

Returning to the truck Paul insisted that the Mwami had confirmed the interview. Mark grumbled all the way back to the *chefferie*. The *chefferie* office was closed. Mark and Paul walked about the building, peering into windows. I assume that once I was out of sight, Paul whispered, *"Monsieur, si tu as besoin d'un representant à Bukavu. . ."* Whatever he suggested, Mark walked off. Paul shrugged.

Out of nowhere appeared an old man with two missing teeth and a narrow beard that dropped from his ears to follow the line of his chin. Veins stood out on his forehead. He demanded to know why the men were peering through the *chefferie* office windows.

Not one to tolerate questions, Mark demanded to know if the man

Reaching Lake Kivu, we passed small beaches with huts crowding the shore. Pirogues cut slowly through the water. Trees bent toward the lake, their leaves drooping into the water.

was a *chefferie* clerk. The old man refused to admit that he was. However, he wore an evident badge of rank: an old tuxedo jacket with black satin lapels.

Mark exploded at the man. If the Mwami did not want to be interviewed, why didn't he just say so?

The tuxedoed clerk exploded back. Everyone, he insisted, must arrange interviews with the Mwami, in advance, by writing.

"How many days in advance?" Mark asked.

The clerk answered in an incomprehensible approximation of French.

"*Deux jours?*" Mark repeated.

"*Oui, deux jours!*" the clerk snapped back.

"*Ou est-ce dix jours?*" I had heard ten days.

"*Mais oui!*" exclaimed the clerk. "*Dix jours!*"

"*Dix-deux jours,*" I said.

"*Deux-dix jours,*" said Mark.

As we headed back down the mountain. Mark said "This fucking

Africa! Nothing works. The people are ignorant, primitive, stupid." He had seen the Mwami, but had not spoken to him. Was there a story in that?

"What the fuck's gonna happen here?" he asked. He leaned his head against the seat and tried to concoct a way to write up an interview that had not taken place. He'd do something. Relate the "wild and bloody saga" of the Mwami's beheadings, of his burying his tribesmen up to their ears. Call the old fraud "a tribal despot." That'd show him.

When we drove through Bagira, children again recognized the film van. They shouted, "See-nay-ma! See-nay-ma!" Paul leaned out of the window to wave.

Reaching Lake Kivu, we passed small beaches with huts crowding the shore. Pirogues cut slowly through the water. Trees bent toward the lake, their leaves drooping into the water. Across the lake blue-gray silhouettes of mountains rose tall and misty in the far distance. Islands seemed to float on the lake, not as distinct shapes, but as blue patterns. Above them cumulus clouds, blue-black, the elephants of the sky, marched along. Water stretched between the film truck and the islands, some of it dark, reflecting the clouds, patches of it silvered by the sun.

"Fucking Africa?" I thought. "Oh, no!" It was so beautiful! I wondered what mysteries dwelt on those islands. What adventure beckoned from the mountains? Then I understood that the islands, the mountains, the clouds were not realities at all. They were dreams, yearnings that nature had given blue shapes. They were longings set across an uncrossable stretch of dark and silvered water. They were out of reach like the Mwami, like all dreams.

Kivu Safari

UREAUCRATIC ALARMS SOUNDED when I had been in Bukavu only about six weeks. This was just as I began to feel that the cultural center and the films program were operating effectively again. The reason for the alarm? It turned out that USIS' parent, the Information Agency in Washington, had misinformed Congress about progress at USIS Coquilhatville in the northwestern Congo. It had reported that an officer was on the ground there.

Not only that but that he had established a cultural center, a tiny light in the Great Darkness of the jungle. And not only that, but that from this small outpost against Communist encroachment on the Dark Continent he was now providing information about Freedom and Democracy to black masses yearning to breathe free.

None of this was true. Did it matter? The Agency was having a very difficult time finding officers who would serve in the Congo. Yes, it mattered because an obscure Congressional staffer might discover the facts. That staffer might jump to the conclusion that USIA had intentionally misled the Congress. Charges of bad faith might fly. So instructions went out from USIA: "Get a body into Coquilhatville." The body was mine. USIS Léo instructed me to leave Bukavu ASAP.

Aware that I might never again find myself so close to East Africa, I requested leave. I yearned to visit the game parks of Kenya and Tanzania. I regarded their animals as the great wonder of the natural world. My bosses denied the request. A USIS body in Coquilhatville had become a matter of urgency.

I felt very disheartened and communicated this feeling to the consul. He smiled with the canniness that was one of the qualities that fitted him for his position. He and his family were taking a weekend trip to Usumbura, the capital of neighboring Burundi, he told me. They would be gone three days. Charley, the consulate's communications man, in whose apartment I lived, would have few duties that weekend.

"Charley needs to get out of town," the consul said.

Charley had been seeing Chantal, a blonde twenty-one-year-old

Goma lay at the north end of Lake Kivu. From Goma we could dash up to Parc National Albert, the Congo's premier game reserve. . . . Few tourists had visited the park since independence. "You'd have the place to yourselves," the consul said.

Belgian girl whose mother was trying to find her a husband. Since I roomed with Charley, I knew that the relationship had become passionate. Charley had told me, "I wouldn't want my Mom to know what I do with that heifer." (Charley invariably referred to young women as "heifers.")

Late one evening while maneuvering Chantal into an accessible position, Charley had removed the knob on the truck's gearshift. In his passion he threw it out the window. The next step would be for him to sneak Chantal into an apartment called the "Commo room" some evening. That might affect security.

The consul's wife worried about his susceptibility to Chantal's wiles. Even Mlle Moutarde, the consul's Belgian secretary who lived with Bukavu's Volkswagen dealer, warned of the spider web being spun by Chantal's mother, Mme DeTree.

"Why don't you take the film truck to Goma?" the consul suggested with a grin. "I'd like to know how that road is, but I sure don't want to test it myself."

Goma lay at the north end of Lake Kivu. From Goma we could dash up to Parc National Albert, the Congo's premier game reserve. I could see elephants and hippos, maybe even lions. My masters in Léo who had denied my leave request need never know of the trip. If they discovered it, I could claim to have been making contacts for program activities.

Few tourists had visited the park since independence. "You'd have the place to yourselves," the consul said.

That night I found Charley in the Bodega restaurant, sitting alone at a table. He was deeply pissed off. Chantal was supposed to meet him. She had stood him up. Since he was on his third beer, drowsiness had begun to dissipate his anger.

"Maybe it's for the best," I said when he told me what was wrong. "Easier to escape the spider web."

"I'm not caught in any spider web," Charley said. "And I won't be any time soon. That bitch."

"Why don't we go up to Goma this weekend?" I suggested. I laid out the plan for him.

"Bitch," Charley grumbled. It was all he said. We ordered dinner.

Soon Chantal entered the Bodega. She joined us without being invited and sat beside Charley. "I'm mad at you," he snarled. The beer-induced drowsiness had disappeared.

"I thought we were meeting at the *Cercle Sportif*," Chantal pleaded. She rubbed her breast against his arm.

"Get lost," Charley said. "I'll see ya sometime." Chantal smiled. She brushed his hair away from his forehead. "Who brought you up here?" Charley asked. "Some guy?"

"*Maman*," she said.

Then, as if on cue, Mme DeTree entered the restaurant. When she saw Charley, she mock-scolded him. "You Americans! You expect Chantal to hunt all over town for you?" Madame sashayed to us and stood behind Charley, her hands on his shoulders. He was undeniably good-looking, black Irish, with the innocent American openness that baffled Europeans.

Mama DeTree possessed a roguish charm. She had some talent as an artist and pretended to be one. Her husband, a bland bucket of incompetence, spent his time drinking at the sports club. In her studio Mama DeTree displayed nude studies of a succulent Chantal. Any prospective suitor knew what was on offer there.

But was she consciously weaving a web? I doubted that. She was shrewd enough to see that even in the present uncertain times the blonde, buxom, compliant and rather pretty Chantal could do better than an American with that guilelessness Europeans mocked and distrusted. In these times of uncertainty she just wanted her daughter to have a little fun. She left her daughter with us.

When our dinners arrived, Chantal nibbled off Charley's plate. He fed her a bite or two with his fork. She grinned at him. He moved his jaw around, trying to suppress the answering smile that was on his lips. "I guess I've got to take you home, don't I?" Charley said. He looked at me. "Can I borrow the film truck?"

I gave him the keys.

After a moment he told Chantal, "I can't see you this weekend. We're going to Goma." He looked at me. "Paul has to go with us," he said. "I'm not going on that road without Paul."

Nor would I go there without Paul. The trip definitely required a Congolese. The unpaved road followed the west bank of the lake. It was treacherously pot-holed and ill maintained. If we needed help from villagers along the way, one of us had better be able to talk to them.

By now, Paul and I had learned how not to get in each other's way. When I tightened discipline on small matters, he was shrewd enough

Goma lay at the north end of Lake Kivu. From Goma we could dash up to Parc National Albert, the Congo's premier game reserve. I could see elephants and hippos, maybe even lions.

to play for the big score. That was travel. There was per diem in that for him—and an even bigger plus. While I wanted to see new country, Paul wanted to meet new women.

Paul could hardly contain his glee when I broached the idea of a trip to Goma. His face burst into a joyful grin, the whites of his eyes and the whites of his teeth sparkling in his dark face. With an air of great importance he immediately set about making preparations. He telephoned Goma's luxurious colonial era hostelry, the Hotel des Grands Lacs, and shouting into the receiver made reservations for *Monsieur l'Attaché du Consulat Américain.*

Besides hoping to see animals and new country, I had another reason for visiting Goma. Shortly before going overseas, I had met Murielle, a Belgian girl raised on a plantation at Saké, only a few miles south of Goma. We had assumed any emotional attachment would be fleeting— after all, I was departing soon for Belgium—but we had fallen in love. I gave a great deal of thought to our marrying. There were, however, issues between us: a difference in religion and questions about how children would be raised. These never got resolved. In fact, because the time was so short once we grew serious, they were hardly discussed.

Gradually we stopped writing during my year-long tour in Brussels. However, once I was assigned to the Congo the correspondence resumed—with enough interest on both sides that I felt it would be wise to *dire bonjour* to her parents.

The consul and his family left for Usumbura at 9:00 o'clock on Friday. We departed for Goma at noon. It rained off and on all day. We left the paved road thirty-five kilometers out, drove past clusters of banana-frond huts, away from the lake and back beside it, climbed the escarpment. Almost at the top, we stopped to stretch. When we were ready to start again, the battery was dead. Ugh.

We rolled the truck backwards and started in compression in reverse. We drove on, up the escarpment and down it. The motor kept cutting out. As long as we were on an incline, we could restart it in compression. Finally the motor died as we moved along the water's edge. Two of us got out. We pushed the truck, but could not move it fast enough to restart it. The rain began again. We corralled a passing African, a banana frond over his head as a rain hat. He helped us push, again in vain.

A European came along. Using bush ingenuity, we restarted the truck by putting the battery from his Land Rover onto our mount. Once the motor was running, we reinstalled our battery; all while the engine was turning.

We went on. The rain grew heavier. We stalled again. Light was fading from the sky. Paul went to find help. Charley and I waited in the truck, grateful that we had recruited Paul. We wondered if there was room for three of us in the truck if we had to spend the night there.

Paul returned shortly with two Europeans: a planter in a slicker, his trousers rolled-up, a woman's plastic fold-up rain scarf on his head, and a Brit who worked at a Lipton Congo plantation near Goma. The Brit pushed us with his Land Rover. We got started again in compression. The hospitable Brit offered to follow us as far as his turn-off and we found that it was not difficult to keep the truck running in second gear.

We drove on through darkness and rain. Suddenly the Brit's headlights were no longer behind us. There was no way to thank him for sparing us a night in the truck.

At Saké we hit pavement again. I peered into the blackness, but I

The bar was devoid of atmosphere. The room was stuffy and smelled of beer. The light was so bright that we needed safari hats and sunglasses. . . . The men sat on one side of the room, the women on the other. . . . Soon a candidate approached. She was very pretty with lustrous skin, flashing eyes, and a bad case of the giggles.

could not make out any turn-off to the plantation where Murielle had grown up.

We knew we were approaching Goma when we saw the red glow atop Nyiragongo, the active volcano that sits behind the town. There were gorillas in those mountains. Wow! The next day we might see elephants and lions, hippos and gazelles! What heaven!

The Hotel des Grands Lacs was splendid. We showered and met for dinner. Throughout the meal Paul was restless. He could not wait to hit a nightclub. I wanted to be rested for the next day's animals and tried to beg off. Paul insisted that we accompany him.

He led us to a brightly-lit room in a building on the main street. When he made his entrance, I understood why it was important that we accompany him. He was a Big Man with Big Friends. The *copain* of white men, he shook hands with everyone, explaining to all that we came from Bukavu and had just dined at the Hotel des Grands Lacs where we were staying.

The bar was devoid of atmosphere. The room was stuffy and smelled of beer. The light was so bright that we needed safari hats and sunglasses. Stick-figure paintings adorned the walls. Crudely-made wooden tables and chairs circled a dance floor. But although music played, a steady cha-cha beat, no one danced.

The men sat on one side of the room, the women on the other. It was like Miss Ryan's dance lessons I had attended at a time when I knew next to nothing about what was clearly on the minds of those sizing each other up across the room. Congolese men sat stolidly at their tables with tall brown bottles of Primus beer before them. They eyed the predatory females who sat across the room, measuring their victims.

Most women—girls really, some no older than middle teens—wore Congolese dress: elaborately tied head cloths, bodices of patterned material, cloths tied about the hips with second cloths draped to emphasize the size and succulence of those hips. Others wore European clothes.

The women knew why men came to the bar: to find a companion for the night. But Charley and me? It was not clear to them—nor perhaps to us—why we were there. Had we come for companions? Or merely to credential Paul?

But it was obvious why Paul had come: to spend money, to make an impression, to carry off the best-looking girl in the place. Soon a candidate approached. She was very pretty with lustrous skin, flashing eyes, and a bad case of the giggles. She was *clad à la européenne*: a white dress with large blue polka dots and a tight waist displaying a body that had not yet begun to thicken. In the light of the room her aureole of combed-out hair shined like a gray mist about her head.

She slid onto Paul's lap. She put an arm around his shoulder. She kissed his cheek. Paul smiled. He gave Charley and me a what-can-I-do?-shrug and became as giggly as she was.

Charley watched Paul getting the Big Man treatment. I wondered if he wanted it, too. Charley had boasted to me that he and Paul had gone "girling" together before I arrived even though their friendship lacked a common language.

Charley spoke no French, Paul no English. Their conversations were uncomplicated. Charley would mime holding a Primus bottle by its

Soon we saw a herd of about fifteen grazing elephants, females with young. Then at the distance of about twenty-five yards we came upon a lone bull.

neck, bringing it to his mouth and tilting his head backwards as if to drink. "Primus. Mademoiselle," he would say to Paul. Paul would answer: "Let's go!"

"I don't know about you," I said, "but I came to see animals."

"Not heifers," Charley said. "At least not these heifers."

We left Paul to be the Big Man in Goma and walked back to the hotel.

The battery repaired, we headed out of Goma through slowly rising countryside, watching three volcanoes jut into clouds. We traveled through country given over to tea, coffee, banana, and quinine plantations. Paul was dressed like a mwami, in office slacks, a tie, and a French-cuff shirt. Charley and I wore jeans.

We reached Parc National Albert in the early afternoon, coming off the Rift Valley escarpment from Rutshuru and moving out onto a long, wide, seemingly empty plain. In some places grass grew higher than our heads.

We drove beside a flat-bottomed stream that cut across a rust- and dark orange-colored gulch through the plain. Paul claimed to have sighted hippos in his binoculars. Oh, sure. We stopped. Damned if he wasn't right. Hippos! Excitement overtook us, the elation of kids. We drove close to their wallow, jumped out of the truck, and gawked at them.

The creatures luxuriated in mud. They seemed a cross between rubberized pigs and Michelin-man horses. From the water in which they stood, they watched us, a mother nuzzling her young one. Sometimes one of them would arch back its neck and open a gigantic pink mouth. Each jaw had the shape of a huge guitar. "Ho, Mama!" Charley said. "Those jaws could take a fender off this truck!"

As we crossed a bridge into Ruindi Camp, a tree burst suddenly into life. Branches waved. Leaves rustled. Baboons! The road jumped alive with creatures scurrying in all directions. Hairy, suspicious faces turned around to observe us across hairy backs. Those backs ended in hairless rumps of shiny leather.

We were the only guests at Ruindi, probably the only guests for weeks. We got our cabins, put our duffels inside, engaged a guide, and returned to the film truck for a late afternoon game run.

The best view was from the top of the truck. We three took turns sitting there. It gave us a view of the entire plain. Soon we saw a herd of

Antelopes watched us. Some, possibly elands, were tawny in color with spiraling horns. Others, topis, stood with their front legs seeming half again the length of their back ones, their hides red and black. When they ran from us, the difference in leg size produced a strange, yet graceful stride.

about fifteen grazing elephants, females with young. Then at the distance of about twenty-five yards we came upon a lone bull.

I was sitting atop the truck and watched him with amazement. At that range the animal seemed enormous, even in the immensity of the plain with mountains rising all around us to the west, with Lake Edward shimmering off to the east. I felt awe at being so close to the elephant. We did not interest him. He observed us and moved off.

The grass began to sway. Pig snouts appeared at the front of these waves of motion, erect tails at the end of them. Wart hogs scampered into view, their ears and long tails lifted to the sky. They trotted in a businesslike way, then turned toward us to back into their holes. Large tusks sprouted from their snouts. They'd win no beauty contests, but the way they trotted, the tufts on their tails raised like flags, delighted me.

We drove on. Antelopes watched us. Some, possibly elands, were tawny in color with spiraling horns. Others, topis, stood with their front legs seeming half again the length of their back ones, their hides red and black. When they ran from us, the difference in leg size produced a strange, yet graceful stride. We saw monkeys and more baboons, waterbuck and more hippos. And Cape buffalo with their wide boss of horns. *"Ce sont très dangereux,"* murmured the guide, eyeing them carefully. ("Very dangerous!")

Charley was driving. Paul and I surveyed the world from our cushions atop the cab of the truck. Suddenly we spotted a huge shape in a mud hole, only large enough to contain this shape. It emerged, a huge hippo, freshly coated in mud. It moved off, glinting in the sun, a plodding blob of light and liquid earth.

We reached the shore of Lake Edward. We stopped, left the truck, and stretched. We watched waterbuck and pelicans and bathing hippos. Monkeys frolicked on the beach. Fish eagles perched in the tops of trees. Paul peered into the distance and pointed off along the lake shore. "There's a commercial fishery over there," he said. "Vitshumbi. An interesting place to visit." I would not look. I did not want to see it. I did not want to think about the works of man. I had come to commune with nature.

Alas! The game run had to end. It was well after 5:00. Here, a mere handful of miles south of the Equator, sundown always fell promptly at

We relaxed on the porch, chatting and relieved that we had escaped. The motor of an invisible boat fishing out in the lake sounded. It was using the village lights to steer by. Wallowing hippos grunted nearby. A pair of them waddled ashore below the house. Villagers shooed them away.

6:00. We started back toward Ruindi. We moved slowly along a track that led beside Lake Edward. We were between the lake and, fifty yards off, a dozen hippos lolling in a wallow.

Charley braked at the edge of a questionable section. It had rained the day before. Mud was everywhere. He hesitated before a patch of it. He consulted the guide. The guide urged him forward. Charley started across the mud. Five feet into it, the truck sank. It settled to its axles in mud.

"*Ooo-la-la!*" Paul exclaimed. We climbed down from the top of the cab. Charley got out, insisting that the guide had assured him the truck could get across.

"You think the guide does a lot of driving?" I asked.

"Thank God, the truck has four-wheel drive," Charley said.

"Yeah, we're lucky." I gestured him to return behind the wheel.

"You know how to use four-wheel drive, right?" he said.

"No."

"Me neither."

Paul who used the truck more than anyone was also ignorant about four-wheel drive.

There was nothing to do but push. Charley, the guide, and I shoved mightily. Paul stood off to the side so that his mwami clothes would not get soiled. Despite our efforts, the truck only settled deeper into mud.

The sun was moving behind the mountains. Charley and I scurried about, uprooting marsh grass and breaking up a small tree, trying to find anything that would give the tires some purchase. The immaculate Paul kept his distance. He shouted suggestions. The guide feigned efforts to help us, but kept his eyes on the hippo wallow. *"C'est très dangereux,"* he said again. Nothing was supposed to block hippos' access to water. We continued to push at the truck. But nothing worked. It was stuck fast.

Light was disappearing from the sky. Our options were not attractive. We could not hike back to Ruindi Camp. It was too far. Before long the coming night would engulf us in a blackness so deep we could see nothing. Wild animals, however, could see us.

It was unlikely that anyone from camp would search for us. The camp staffers had no vehicles. We could spend the night in the truck, hoping that curious hippos did not push it over. Or we could try to reach the fishery at Vitshumbi. Before I had refused to look at it. Now I was grateful it was so near. With luck we might get there before nightfall. With luck angry hippos would not come after us.

We started for the fishing village. How far was it? Less than two miles? Should we run? Could we? Suddenly hippos began to grunt. They surrounded us. There was no cover, no trees to climb. So we ran. And walked. Walked and ran. We hoped that hippos, which have bad eyesight, would lose us in the twilight.

Darkness descended. Lights came on at Vitshumbi. We hurried toward them, walking, running. We were breathing hard by the time we came to mud-and-wattle huts. We trudged more confidently as we passed permanent one-room structures. A hippo wandered in the village street. A fisherman waved it back toward the water. Villagers looked up from cook fires. A hippo loose in the village did not surprise them, but four spooked figures stumbling out of the darkness did.

Paul asked to see the director of the fishery. An African led us toward a lighted building. Its porch overlooked the lake. On the peak of its roof perched half a dozen marabou storks.

On the porch sat a group of people having *apéritifs*: a Belgian of middle age and a family of East Indians. The Belgian stood squinting as we came out of the darkness. An Indian woman, enough younger than the Belgian to be his daughter, rose to her feet. She was a quietly attractive girl, slender, but full-breasted. In the dim light and for smelly, deserted, end-of-the-world Vitshumbi she was very beautiful. I knew that Charley was thinking "Heifer! Heifer!"

We all stared at one another. Then Paul laughed. *"Ah! C'est toi!"* he exclaimed. ("It's you!") The Belgian studied him, then grinned and stuck out his hand. *"Tu habite ici, eh?"* Paul asked, using the familiar form. ("You live here, do you?")

"Qu'est ce que tu fais ici?" the Belgian asked, responding in the familiar form. ("What are you doing here?") He and Paul shook hands.

During *"les troubles,"* when the Kivu was in turmoil immediately after independence, the Belgian had needed to flee. Paul rowed him across Lake Kivu to safety in Rwanda. Now the Belgian introduced his wife, the beautiful young woman. Her family was visiting, she explained. She offered us drinks.

We relaxed on the porch, chatting and relieved that we had escaped. The motor of an invisible boat fishing out in the lake sounded. It was using the village lights to steer by. Wallowing hippos grunted nearby. A pair of them waddled ashore below the house. Villagers shooed them away.

The Belgian offered to let us use the fishery's large Volvo truck. He had it brought around for us. We headed back into the park, accompanied by a dozen villagers. Certainly now we would extricate the film truck.

We took a dry route to reach it. Paul directed the expedition, drawing on night-driving experience gained in cruising nighttime Bukavu. We passed indistinguishable animal shapes. A tree that moved turned out to be an elephant. We caught the glowing eyes of animals in our headlights. The driver extinguished them when the animals charged.

We caught sight of the film truck in the Volvo's headlights. As we neared it, the Volvo slid around in mud. My heart sank. Could the Volvo get stuck? Was Paul really the man to be in charge? The Volvo sank for a moment, but moved on. Once again we came close to getting stuck.

I shouted at the top of my voice, *"C'est fini pour ce soir!"* ("It's finished for tonight!") I would not risk miring the Volvo truck. *"C'est fini! C'est fini!"* All of us returned to Ruindi camp.

We had locked our cabins well and had left the keys to them in the film truck. We bedded down in other quarters in muddy underwear.

I did not sleep. I stared at the night. I said prayers and wondered what would happen if we could not rescue the film truck. Would leaving it stuck in Parc Albert cost me my job? How would Léo react to learning that I'd gone dancing off to see animals when I had been specifically instructed not to? Would I be sent home from Africa in disgrace?

At dawn the Volvo took all of us back out to the film truck. With fishery men to help us use long planks for traction, we rescued it from mud in short order. We thanked our helpers and sent them back to Vitshumbi.

I'd escaped! Léo need never know I'd been to Parc Albert! I was so elated that I was ready for another game run, for the circuit where we could see lions. But Charley had had enough. Paul was anxious to return to the arms of his blue polka-dotted *amie*. We drove back silently to Goma. We reached the Hotel des Grands Lacs by noon.

The following afternoon Charley drove us home—all too quickly. Paul had reconnected with the young woman in the blue polka dot dress. A night of passion had left him tired and speechless. His friend had so extracted the juices from him that halfway down the lake he insisted we stop at a plantation house. He ordered an African there to fetch him a glass of water. Charley was equally quiet, thinking probably of Chantal awaiting him in Bukavu. I contented myself with wondering if there would be a letter for me from Murielle DeMunck.

We stayed in second gear until well within sight of Bukavu. The streets were deserted. A rumor had spread that the Mwami of Kabare might stir up trouble, perhaps even send warriors to invade the town. Where usually the night was full of cha-cha rhythms from Congolese bars, this night there was only silence.

Bukavu Again

WHEN I RETURNED TO BUKAVU fifteen months later after serving in Coquilhatville, many things had changed. But Paul Wemboyendja still had great contacts and still was chasing women. And I still wanted to see some country.

What had changed? There was a new consul, a single man divorced from a French woman, who had started his overseas career with USAID in Vietnam. Two American officers now staffed the cultural center. The departing Public Affairs Officer, whom I replaced on temporary duty, had extended USIS functions about as far as possible in and around Bukavu. Paul Polakoff, the information officer, published a bulletin in French each weekday, taking its contents from Voice of America radio transmissions. It went to 450 recipients and was read twice over Radio Bukavu in French and Swahili.

The Simba Rebellion had gripped the Congo. Although it showed no signs of combat, Bukavu had been a battleground. Pockets of rebels were still operating in parts of the Kivu. An American lieutenant colonel, maybe forty-five, and a translator / driver half his age were now stationed at the Consulate to advise the local ANC commander who wanted no advice.

Because Bukavu was still considered dangerous—no American woman could serve there—most of these men bunked in the consul's house where I had lived when I first served in Bukavu, fresh from Brussels. A contingent of CIA officers had moved into the house next door.

Shortly after I returned, the consul wanted to travel to Goma at the north end of Lake Kivu. His purpose was to discourage American missionaries from returning to isolated stations until the rebellion was in hand. He suggested that I might like to drive the film truck in tandem with him.

USIS Léopoldville had produced a film showing the central government's attack on the rebel stronghold at Stanleyville. It was to be given the widest possible distribution.

"You up for a trip to Goma?" I asked Paul Wemboyendja.

"Ah, oui, Monsieur. Bien sur!" he replied with an enormous grin.

"Are there places beyond Goma where we could go?"

At this question Paul's grin grew even broader. "We could do several showings in Goma," he suggested. "Hit Gisenyi in Rwanda. Even Vitshumbi if you want to go that far." His eyebrows oscillating, he laughed at the mention of the Lake Edward fishing village.

We began to plan a major foray north of Goma.

Wherever we went our truck would be loaded with appropriate gear for showing films. We would carry two projectors with loud-speakers, a portable screen, a generator, the films themselves, four jerry cans of gasoline, two of water. We would also take along two canvas pouch bags of the USIS publication Perspectives Américaines, twelve stacks of Nouveaux Horizon books for schools, three small boxes of pamphlets plus a carton of NH biographies of President Lyndon Johnson for government leaders.

Since I had returned only recently to the Kivu, I let Paul propose the film show sites. He suggested two to six locations in and around Goma, the area's largest town. Nearby was Kiretshe-Saké, the seat of the provincial government of North Kivu. Farther afield lay Rumangabe, the site of an ANC camp; Jemba where there was a Catholic secondary school; the town of Rutshuru; possibly Ruindi camp in Parc Albert where Paul and I had lodged on our Kivu safari; and the Vitshumbi fishing camp. Those were Paul's suggestions.

Paul and I consulted a map. "What about Lubero, Butembo, and Beni?" I asked.

I had heard the consul whispering with the CIA boys about an operative at work in Beni. I thought it might be interesting to take a look at the place.

Paul shrugged.

"We might even go as far as the Ruwenzoris," I said. "Make a side trip to the Ituri forest." I had recently read Colin Turnbull's *The Forest People.*

Paul laughed because this was clearly getting out of hand. "You want to show films to pygmies?"

"I understand there are some gorgeous pygmy girls." I mentioned as a sweetener, "You'd have something to boast about when you got back to Bukavu."

Paul looked interested and laughed.

"What I really want to do," I admitted, "is to get to the source of the

Semliki Nile on the north bank of Lake Edward." Huge herds of hippos were said to graze there. The idea of watching a thousand hippos at one time inflamed my imagination.

"You're talking several weeks," Paul said.

"Maybe a month. We'd have to carry food." I was not an adventures-in-eating traveler. Probably I would not want to eat what Africans ate— unless I got very, very hungry.

"What if the truck broke down?" Paul asked. "What if we got stuck?" He was recalling our adventures on the Kivu safari.

"I'd really like to do this," I said.

"I would like to go to Paris," replied Paul.

"We'll do this first."

Paul laughed at my insane desire to play Livingston, Speke, and Burton rolled into one.

When I broached my idea of the film trip to USIS Léopoldville, I was told that rebel activity north of Beni required cancellation of any ideas about Lubero-Butembo-Beni. The consul doubted that our vehicle could reach the source of the Semliki Nile. ANC soldiers were shooting at anything that moved near Lake Edward. That eliminated Vitshumbi as well. "For the time being," decided the consul, "maybe Goma is as far north as you should go." Including two days travel, that would mean a trip of less than a week.

Then at breakfast one morning the consul announced that the new prime minister of Burundi, a Hutu friendly to the West, had been assassinated. The assassin had shot him outside a hospital where he'd just visited his wife and newborn baby. With that development the consul postponed his plans for the trip.

But Paul Wemboyendja and I did get away. Our first day's drive to Goma was pleasant, the lake enthralling as always. It was the short dry season, late January. A haze covered the lake. As we approached Goma which sits on the extreme eastern edge of an 1889 volcanic eruption, the volcanoes behind the town revealed themselves only sporadically.

I looked forward to stopping at the Hotel des Grands Lacs. But the town was busy when we arrived. It stayed that way throughout our visit. An Air Congo flight had been canceled. Its passengers filled the hotel to capacity.

"If you like," suggested the receptionist, "try again tomorrow."

That evening Paul and I drove down to Saké. A rather grubby collection of shanties, it was a marked contrast to our previous evening in the former governor's palace.

"I will. You can count on that!"

Paul chose to stay in Goma at a Congolese pension where he was known and welcomed by *la patronne*. He may have spent previous nights with her. I found lodging across the Rwanda border in Gisenyi. I had thought we might show films that night in Goma. But because the border closed at 6:00, that was not possible.

The next morning I was able to get rooms for Paul and me in the Hotel des Grands Lacs. When I connected with Paul, we decided to organize a special showing that evening. Since our information goal was to bolster Congolese confidence in US military backing for the central government, the program would consist of the USIS Léo production about US paratroops dropping into Stanleyville and another USIS film discussing the American defense system and its worldwide commitments.

To organize the showing, we visited the Léo-appointed *Commissaire Général Extraordinaire*. On behalf of the central government, he was charged with maintaining law and order in the territories of Goma and Rutshuru. Although claimed by the province of North Kivu, these territories refused to join it. The *Commissaire* was happy to help us. He even agreed that we should hold the showing at his residence, the former home of the Belgian governor.

Paul and I divided tasks. With the help of the North Kivu information man, Paul prepared invitations, devised a guest list, submitted it to the *Commissaire* for approval, and delivered the invitations.

I checked into the hotel and toted information materials into my room. There I assembled seventy info packets for our guests. Each one included USIS pamphlets, a *Nouveaux Horizons* book, and a copy of President Lyndon Johnson's inaugural address, rated only C+ by the consul. Some of the NH books were Johnson biographies. The story of his hard-won rise from Texas dirt farmers might give hope to ambitious members of the Congolese elite.

Our morning chores done, Paul and I descended on the *Commissaire's* residence in the afternoon to rearrange furniture, transforming the parlor into a theater, and set up our equipment. We returned at 6:45 to welcome guests. The *Commissaire* himself was down at the border, trying to convince border guards to allow the Prefect of Gisenyi cross to attend the show. They refused.

The showing began well. Then Paul rolled a film I introduced as *Pour Maintenir la Paix* (To Maintain Peace) about American defense capabilities. On the screen flashed the words: *"La Visite de Monsieur Houphet-Boigny à Washington."* ("Houphet-Boigny's Visit to Washington") What? It was a newsreel, the wrong film. I blurted: *"Je vous prie de nous excuser, Messieurs-Dames. Nous allons arrêter la séance pendant quelques minutes."* (Please excuse us. We'll stop the show for a few minutes.)

The wrong film! How had that happened? I had expressly told Paul to check the films before we left Bukavu. Now I was annoyed at myself for not checking them myself. Apparently films borrowed over the weekend had been replaced in the wrong cans.

But this was the Congo. The audience could not have been less concerned. Mistakes were part of the developing world. Everyone took them in stride. Our audience had seen few films recently and were happy with whatever we showed them.

I reported to my masters in Léo that the evening had been an information triumph. In a matter of ten hours and without prior arrangement we set up a dignitaries showing of our films. We gathered several dozen of the most important Congolese of Goma and North Kivu. We showed them films, chatted them up, and placed USIS info packets in their hot little hands.

The next morning we showed films in several auditoriums. These were easy to set up. Nothing needed to be done by prior arrangement. That afternoon while Paul drove the film truck around town, announcing our evening show through loudspeakers, I crossed back over to Gisenyi for a swim in Lake Kivu. It was impossible to swim at Bukavu due to bilharzia (parasitic flatworms) problems, but entirely safe, I was assured, in Gisenyi. How refreshing it was!

That evening Paul and I drove down to Saké. A rather grubby collection of shanties, it was a marked contrast to our previous evening in the former governor's palace. We arrived at the soccer field to find the viewing stand choked with Congolese. Milling youngsters filled the playing field, all of them excited, some frenzied, at the prospect of movies.

As we entered the field, kids surrounded the film truck, screaming, dancing, gyrating, yelling, "See-nay-ma! See-nay-ma!" Paul laughed with his usual delight.

We thought our audience would number 500. It looked like the crowd might exceed 2,000. We were the biggest attraction the town had seen in months. The audience's excitement empowered Paul. Because clouds were gathering ominously, it disconcerted me.

"These folks look pretty wound up," I observed to Paul. "We gonna be able to handle them?"

"No problem!" he delightedly replied, energized by their anticipation.

"What if it rains?"

What indeed! The sky grew dark. The temperature fell. Wind came up. Droplets wet our faces. We repacked the equipment we'd already unloaded. We took refuge in the cab of the truck to see what happened.

The droplets became a downpour. Curtains of raindrops fell on the field, slowly at first, then in torrents. The crowd ran for the viewing pavilion. They overwhelmed it with bodies. Unlike Americans, Congolese did not object to their private space being invaded and kids piled on top of each other. I hoped no one would be trampled.

As Paul and I watched through the downpour, the pavilion became a breathing creature. First it would push out like a body gasping for air. That was humanity at the rear of the pavilion pushing forward. People would spill off the pavilion. Then they would hurl themselves back onto it and the body would contract like lungs exhaling.

"We wait, right?" I asked Paul.

"We wait, *Monsieur*."

Rain pelted the field. The air grew colder. The rain turned to hail. It clattered against the viewing stand roof, against the hood of our truck. We sat in the cab, getting ever wetter. We could not possibly drive off the field and disappoint the excited Congolese. There might be a riot in the rain. In any case, we could not see five yards in front of us. We did not know the roads.

There was nothing to do but wait out the downpour. We could not see. We sat, soaking wet. We laughed at our predicament. At the same time I thought: What a damn silly way to earn a living!

When the storm more or less passed, we set up our equipment and showed our films. Did it matter that everybody was wet? No. We showed films until the screen collapsed.

The next day we did four Goma film showings and headed back to Bukavu through central Rwanda. More country to see. Why not take a look? No roads were paved except in the capital Kigali. Heading down on a mountain road, very narrow, we passed an up-coming vehicle so close that its chassis scraped off our outside mirror.

We spent the night at Gabiro at the rest house for Kagera Park, Rwanda's sole game reserve. An Irish couple managed the place and provided quite a tasty dinner, zebra steak. We had topi stew the next day for lunch. Earlier that morning Paul and I toured the park, bringing different mind sets into our game run. When I watched zebra, impala, topi, eland and even bush pigs, I saw only grace, beauty and the freedom of living wild.

"Isn't this fantastic!" I rhapsodized. "What beauty Nature has."

Paul gazed at me skeptically, then looked at the animals. He commented, "Good steaks."

Continuing our travels, Paul and I passed through dense mountain jungle between Butare and Bukavu. The day was cold and misty. The trees grew thicker than I had ever seen them. Batwa—pygmies—lived in that forest. We saw herds of their goats, cattle and pigs and men small of stature tending them. I did not need to go to the Ituri to encounter pygmies.

I was glad to get back to Bukavu. But I never lost my hope to reach the Semliki Nile and see one thousand hippos grazing there.

Jack Parks

J ACK PARKS LIKED TO TALK. The first time I met him, he said: "*Moi*, I'm a Jersey kid. Officially Jacques. French mother who taught me her language. First year in college I'm bored stiff. Bugged out. Joined up to see some combat in 'Nam. Try out the women there. Feel like a man. What the hell happens? I'm sent to fucking Congo, driver / interpreter for a light colonel who's supposed to be advising local dogfaces. Do they want advice? No. Am I gonna see combat? No."

I met him at the consul's house in Bukavu. We were chatting over drinks before going in to dinner. Jack and South Carolina Lt Colonel JD Bryant had arrived that day. They already knew that the local commander of the *Armée Nationale Congolaise* had no interest in the American military nosing around.

"Bryant's a good ole boy," said Parks. "Keeps his own counsel. The JD's for Jeff Davis. Long military heritage. Daddy and Grandaddy officers. Graduated from The Citadel, that whole tribe. Together three weeks. A week in DC, two weeks in Léo. Don't know shit about Africa, neither one of us, but we're here to set things right. There was some fighting here, correct?"

Two months earlier, before I returned to Bukavu from the northwestern Congo, Lumumbist rebels attacked the town, coming north from Uvira and the postage stamp country of Burundi. There American policy makers feared that Chinese Communists had established a base and were training anti-American guerrillas. The ANC blunted the attack and chased the guerrillas—tribesmen was what they really were—back onto the Ruzizi plain. Bukavu was now relatively safe. The local ANC commander, proud of his victory over the rebels, thought Bukavu invincible. He didn't need a corn-pone American colonel and his twenty-year-old driver to tell him what to do.

"How's a fella get laid in this town?" Parks asked. "Looks like it's short of women. You tried African? How's that?" Parks winked at me. "I'm asking for the colonel, you understand. He's the one wants to know."

The consul's house, a mansion built during the Belgian heyday, stood on a bluff overlooking Lake Kivu and its islands with a backdrop of mountains. Parks might wish he were proving himself a real man in Vietnam, but this was unquestionably better duty.

The house was a kind of barracks, more a BOQ really, and had been from the days of the rebel attack. Since the consul did not regard Bukavu as immune from attack in the way the ANC commander did, a number of us were living at the house. Besides the consul and me, lodgers included a radio operator on TDY from Madrid and occasionally the crew of a C-47 that flew intelligence missions over rebel-held areas. Now Parks and Bryant. We each had our own room.

In addition, "agency" men inhabited the house just across the driveway. Frequently all of us dined together. The consul's cook provided us breakfast and dinner. We all chipped in for his services and the food.

Hardly a week after Bryant and Parks arrived, the colonel began to get restless. Since there was little to do at night, I invited them to come along on a film show Paul Wemboyendja and I were giving in Kadutu.

While Paul and I set up the show, Paul playing Congolese cha-cha music from his own recordings, the military pair watched our audience arrive. I noticed Bryant checking out the women. It was not hard to diagnose the restlessness problem.

"Your boss is a little hungry," I commented to Parks.

"The man is starving," he said. "And I'm not much better."

"Wemboyendja could fix him up."

"He's an officer. He wants a blonde."

"He's in Africa."

"He may have tried that while at the Citadel—right of passage stuff. But he's a colonel now. From Carolina. The guy's got standards."

"Where'll he find blondes?"

"He's seen them at the *Cercle Sportif.*" That was a social club, once highly stratified, now open to anyone with white skin. "We've heard there's a real epidemic of hanky-panky."

The consul's house was not a good place for guys assailed by restlessness. It was out of town and little happened there at night. We read. We played chess. We did puzzles. The consul often fell asleep on the couch, only to waken at 1:00 or 2:00 in the morning and make his way carefully upstairs so that he would not grow fully awake.

We were men without women (except those gazing at us out of *Playboy,* that staple of the barracks, and those moving languidly across our memories, thanks to the Italian love songs from the consul's collection).

And except for the evening when his secretary brought him some papers. She was the slim, sophisticated, young Mme Gaillard, a woman of the world in the French style, also very business-like. I had known her the year before as Mlle Moutarde. Now, since she lived with Gaillard, Bukavu's Volkswagen dealer, she was accorded the honorific Mme Gaillard.

Some of us did not much care for Gaillard. We thought he treated her badly, like a baggage. He never referred to her as *ma femme* (in French both my woman and my wife), but always as *mon amie* or *ma copine* (my girlfriend). Given the shortage of women in Bukavu, especially women as attractive as his companion, we felt she deserved respect of the sort we would have willingly given her. Nonetheless, she was single-mindedly crazy about him. She never flirted with any of us. No accounting for taste.

That evening her presence wafted perfume around the room. It stirred up vibrations. She enchanted us first by being female and second by being a woman who followed her desires. At this time before Americans lived together unmarried, her cohabitation with the VW dealer made her seem determined to follow her passions. Their relationship possessed an exotic, ultra European aura.

Joining our circle, Madame picked up a copy of *Playboy*. She cast a critical eye at the nudes and was not impressed.

She demanded, "How can you stand such fleshy women?" We just gazed at her, a woman.

The next afternoon Col Bryant came to see me at the cultural center. Wemboyendja was working at a desk in the office with me. In a rather military way Bryant said, "Could we speak confidentially?"

I sent Wemboyendja on an errand. Judging the way he usually handled errands, he would probably be gone for an hour.

"Last night that Mme Guy—" He stumbled at her name.

"Gaillard."

"Yeah. Savvy woman." I nodded. Finally he said, "I thought maybe she could make some introductions for me. Could you set that up?"

"What would that involve?"

"I'd like to— Uh—" It was hard for him to get the words out. "Consult her about—" He shrugged. "Options. Maybe you could act as an interpreter. I don't want that chatterbox Parks in on this. And I can't very well ask the consul."

I arranged that Col. Bryant and I should call on Mme Gaillard. She arranged to be sick that day, out of the office. She received us in her dressing gown, coughed now and then, and may indeed have been under the weather.

In my best, none too polished, man of the world style, I explained that Monsieur wished to make friends with a woman in town and to visit her occasionally, perhaps in the afternoons. "He understands that virtually all the women in town are married. His visits would be discreet. He does not want to compromise them or his position as a representative of the United States."

"Tout à fait compris," said Mme Gaillard without a blush. ("Completely understood.") I withdrew from the negotiations. Mme Gaillard spoke enough English and Bryant understood enough French so that they could handle the matter from there.

As I understood what happened, Mme Gaillard escorted the colonel through the possibilities. She enumerated local candidates who had adventures and might be open to one with him. They discussed these women, their discretion, their marital entanglements, and the kind of gifts they might want to receive.

When I rejoined them at the end of their discussion, Mme Gaillard shook her head sadly and said, "Hélas! No one." Since Bryant had seemed very determined to have an adventure, I was a little surprised by this development. But perhaps the requirements for discretion could not be met.

A few days later when I was at the consulate, Mme Gaillard asked me, "Have the sittings begun?" I frowned. "For your friend the colonel."

"Sittings?"

"Excusez moi," said Madame, suddenly blushing. "I have spoken out of turn."

I smiled. "The colonel is sitting for his portrait?" I asked. Madame shrugged. "With Mme DeTree? She paints, doesn't she?"

"I really know nothing of the matter."

Bryant was perhaps forty-five. Mme DeTree was nearing fifty, *zaftig*, companionable, and rather witty. I had known her as a sponsor of her daughter Chantal's romance with Charley, the consulate's former radioman. Charley had been transferred to Scandinavia and Chantal was living with relatives in Belgium. I recalled that Madame had a studio in her home and that her husband spent his days playing cards at the *Cercle Sportif.*

Bryant did not talk about his doings. After all who could forget that "Loose lips sink ships"? However, in less than a week he arrived for dinner half an hour late. He was relaxed and mellow. His skin looked as if he'd visited the fountain of youth. Parks examined him carefully across the table and lowered his face to grin.

As we went for drinks in the living room, Parks sidled up to me to whisper. "JD's been on a bombing run."

"Looks like he hit the target."

"And more than once is my guess. Now how do we get me some poon?"

"Our radioman Charley used to go 'girling' with Wemboyendja."

"No shit. I guess that means African."

If we were men without women, we were not without pets: a female puppy that delighted us; a five-year-old cocker spaniel with a bored expression and tired blood that dragged around like a lobotomy victim; a taciturn and ill-tempered parrot that strutted around and occasionally engaged in whistling contests; an antelope banished from the house after the occasion when, displayed to guests, it urinated all over the rug; and most importantly a bush baby.

"What the shit is that?" Parks asked when Bush Baby flew across the room and landed on the consul's shoulder. The consul explained that Bush Baby slept all day and came alive at night, jumping huge distances.

"High-flying, bug-eyed critter," Parks allowed. "Small enough to fit in your hand."

The consul noted that Bush Baby had a drinking problem.

"No shit?" Parks asked. "Daddy must have been a koala bear. Mama was a raccoon and a monkey had been playing around in the wood pile."

"Watch him," the consul said. "If he sees an open bottle he'll fly over to it and lick around the top. Eventually he'll fall asleep against the curtains." The room's curtains hung to the floor. Bush Baby slept there.

On rare occasions Père Nico joined us. He was an Italian priest, about twenty-five, rail thin, bad skin, of very conservative orientation. He wore metal-framed glasses through which he seemed to regard us with disapproval. I had welcomed him several times into the USIS library; he borrowed paperbacks in our simplified *Nouveaux Horizons* collection. He came around to the consul's house not only to practice English

One day when the C-47 was doing a reconnaissance run I flew with it. Nico was along as a spotter. The grass-covered mountains behind Uvira rose abruptly, majestically. Rebels lived hidden among them. Peering below me I could not distinguish the rebel camps. We fired bursts of shots at them and Nico waved his arms approvingly. The rebels returned the fire, trying to down our plane. I laughed at the excitement of that moment.

conversation, but to escape the graybeard priests who had been in Bukavu for decades.

Père Nico hit it off with the guys that flew the C-47. Occasionally they took him along on flights to serve as a spotter. He had worked for a time in Uvira, at the north end of Lake Tanganyika, and knew the territory where rebels had camps in the mountains.

One day when the C-47 was doing a reconnaissance run over that territory, I flew with it. Nico was along as a spotter. The grass-covered mountains behind Uvira rose abruptly, majestically. Rebels lived hidden among them. Flying over the mountains, sitting strapped into the plane's open doorway, I felt I could see the entire world. Peering below me I could not distinguish the rebel camps. We fired bursts of shots at them and Nico waved his arms approvingly. He shouted at me, "We make them shit!" and laughed heartily.

The rebels returned the fire, trying to down our plane. I laughed at the excitement of that moment. Nico grinned and yelled, "Now *we* shit!" I rather liked the guy and was happy to have a European using the library.

But whenever Père Nico visited the house at night, Parks would shake his head after he left. "That ugly guy!" he would say. "Such bad teeth. Priests drag them out of junior high school, especially in poor towns. Seduce them with false promises about a better life. Fill them with conservative claptrap and keep 'em in a cage all their lives. I'll bet that guy's never been laid."

I listened to Parks' assessment.

"Until I met this guy, I thought only American priests were clucks enough to take celibacy seriously. You think this guy's fruity?"

"There may be more balls there than you think," I suggested.

"I don't like the guy. Every time he comes here, I wanta run."

I had seen Parks chatting with Paul Wemboyendja and asked if Paul had put Parks on to things in Bukavu the consul might not recommend.

"African night clubs," Parks said. "Meat markets. Hothouses for VD. I'm hanging out these days at the *Cercle Sportif*."

"Anything going on down there?"

He gave me an enormous wink. "Too early to say." That was a most reserved comment from this loquacious guy. I figured something truly earth-shaking must be in the works.

One night Père Nico came to the house well after dinner, looking deeply shaken. When he arrived, the consul was napping on the couch. Nico got a whiskey and woke him. The consul sat up, looking annoyed at being disturbed. "Victor is no more," he said. Victor was his driver.

"What happened?" The consul shook his head to waken.

"He was killed. An ambush. Just south of Kamanyola." Kamanyola had long been a rebel hideout.

"I was supposed to drive the truck he took," the priest said. "It was mere chance I stayed behind." He put his face in his hands, very near to tears. We got some dinner for him.

"Can you stay the night?" the consul asked. Nico looked uncertain, but was clearly tempted. "Stay! Is there bed check for priests?"

Nico laughed at that idea and agreed to stay.

The next day Bryant and Parks accompanied him down to Kamanyola to investigate the ambush. There were no ambushes that day on that road and they were back in time for dinner.

Paul Wemboyendja and I went north for a week to show films at

Goma and Gisenyi across the border in Rwanda. When I returned. Col Bryant looked even more relaxed.

"How are things with your boss?" I asked Parks.

"A-OK," he said. "Sitting for an artist twice a week is good for his disposition."

"You still hanging around the *Cercle*?"

He pulled me aside and spoke softly so that none of the others could here. "Matter of fact," he whispered, "I'm doing a first bombing run tonight."

"Who's your victim?"

He grinned, knowing he should not tell. But he was a man who found his exploits fascinating. He mentioned the target, a longtime *colon's* daughter Minou Morel who lived three houses down the road. I'd seen her biking. She was very scrawny, possibly under age. Parks would meet plenty of bones and angularities in wooing her.

"She's not too young?"

"They start young in Africa."

"But you're a Yank. Be careful."

"She swears she's eighteen. My guess is sixteen."

"My guess is fourteen."

"That's when she lost her cherry. Her cousin took it."

"There'll be a *zamo* outside the house."

"I tip him some CF."

"That easy?"

"She leaves the window open. I crawl in and pleasure her."

"Be careful," I advised. "Charles Morel is a buddy of the consul's. If the consul hears what you're doing, he'll go through the roof."

Parks gave me a wink, confident he could handle the challenge.

We played a couple of games of chess. At 10:00 he gave me the high sign and left. The next morning he slept through breakfast.

Parks danced into my office at the cultural center that afternoon. A grin rode his face. He sat in a chair, spread his legs wide apart to signal he was ready for anything, laced his hands together, and placed them on his stomach. "Man," he said. "Romeo did it. Julien Sorel did it. I did it. You ever read *The Red and the Black*?"

In fact, I had paid my homage to M Stendhal. Sorel had gone through a woman's window without invitation and never looked back.

For a time Parks squirmed through Minou's window every night, returning shortly before dawn to sleep through breakfast. Then one night at dinner the consul asked, "Where the hell do you go every night?"

"Me?" Parks answered.

I was impressed that Parks's French mother's instruction had included such classics.

"Tiptoed through the back yard, trying to get the right window," he said. "Climbed through. Into pitch darkness. It's jumping off a cliff with a stiff dick. Land safe. Hear whispers: *"Cheri! Cheri! Depeche-toi, cheri! 'Suis enflamée!'* ("Hurry! I'm on fire!") Shed duds. Scoot under the net. Falling. Land where it's moist and warm. Ahhhh!" He closed his eyes. An expression of pure contentment spread across his face. "I'm going back tonight."

Whereas the colonel never spoke a word about the art world, his well-being saying it all, Parks was a kiss-and-tell prattler. I supposed he detailed his adventures to Wemboyendja who could savor them with him. He gave me regular *tours d'horizon*.

He crawled through windows to enjoy the body of a teenager about whom he cared not at all while I was waiting for letters from Murielle DeMunck, for the mere joy of savoring her prose.

For a time Parks squirmed through Minou's window every night, returning shortly before dawn to sleep through breakfast. Then one night at dinner the consul asked, "Where the hell do you go every night?"

"Me?" Parks answered. "I'm here."

"Like hell," said the consul. "I climb upstairs in the early hours and sometimes stumble into your room by mistake." Parks's room was a small one next door to that of the consul. "You're not there."

"I must be in the bathroom."

"I don't think so," said the consul,

"He makes reveille," said the colonel coming to Parks' defense.

"You're representing the United States government," the consul said. "Don't forget that."

Once the consul had fallen asleep on the couch, Parks whispered to me, "Oh, shit! He's gonna send me to the stockade. Fatso Judson's waiting for me. You ever read *From Here to Eternity*?"

"Saw the movie."

He began to bite his thumb. "I can't see her tonight. Will you go down and tell her I can't come?"

I laughed aloud. "Are you out of your mind?"

"You won't touch her, though, right?"

"I'm not getting anywhere near her. Telephone her. Haven't you got her number?"

"Her *papa* will answer the phone. That'll queer everything."

Parks stood the girl up. He made sure the consul saw that he was in the house when he made his post-midnight journey upstairs.

Parks sought out Minou the next day at the *Cercle Sportif*, explained the circumstances, begged forgiveness, and agreed to see her again that night. He left about 10:00 and was back by midnight so the consul could check on him. Every few nights he stayed at the consul's house so as not to push his luck. That became the routine.

A more mature lover, the colonel did sittings only in the afternoons and only twice a week. He and his *amie* varied the portraiture schedule so as not to raise suspicions of either the consul or the cuckold.

Unexpectedly the consul caught a ride on a C-130 Hercules *and made a trip to Léopoldville. He would be gone two days. When Parks heard the news, he danced into my office, wearing another of his grins. "Am I gonna surprise my sweetie!"*

Then the consul got a tip that "hostile elements" might attack an American. The warning seemed mischievous, malicious, improbable. Who were the "hostiles" anyway: police? ANC? But the consul took the warning seriously. He put a stop to roaming. All the residents of his house were to be there every night. The colonel instructed Parks to stay in. Worried that an attack against an American would damage his reputation, the consul began to stay up late, sometimes pacing the halls.

Parks rendezvoused with Minou at the *Cercle Sportif* and regretfully informed her that for the time being he could not see her at night. He suggested meeting her in the late afternoons, but she feared her vigilant father. Parks cursed his luck. "She's the one good thing about this place," he told me, almost with tears in his eyes. "If I can't see her, I'm gonna go crazy!"

Then Parks' luck turned. Unexpectedly the consul caught a ride on a C-130 Hercules and made a trip to Léopoldville. He would be gone two days. When Parks heard the news, he danced into my office, wearing another of his grins. "Am I gonna surprise my sweetie!" he exulted. "Gonna stay with her the whole fucking night. And that's exactly what it's gonna be." He gave me the high sign when he left the consul's residence that night about 10:00.

The next morning Parks appeared at breakfast, a very sour expression on his face. I was surprised to see him there. I assumed he'd miss breakfast.

He came to the center that afternoon. "Oh, man," he said. "You're not gonna believe this."

"What happened?"

He shook his head in disgust.

"Is it over with Minou?"

"Maybe. I dunno." He threw himself into a chair. "I'm into her room at 10:10 and outa my clothes. She's surprised to see me, says, 'What're you doing here?' like she wants to get rid of me. But I silence her with kisses. We have incredible passion. That is one warm lady. So I'm holding her, gathering the energy for Number Two. I whisper in her ear. *'Minou, mon petit chou*, have I got a surprise for you. We can do this all night.'

"She sounds alarmed. 'We're in luck,' I say. 'The consul's in Léo. I don't have to go home.'

"'What about the stockade?' she asks. 'What about that Fatso!'

"Isn't that cute? She remembered. And I'm on fire. 'Not going to any stockade,' I assure her. 'Right now I'm taking you to heaven.'

"So I take her again. Never been so good. My hand's over her mouth because she's moaning. And I'm laughing while doing what we're not built to do while laughing. And it's fantastic! Afterwards we're absolutely spent. Blotto. Wasted. I'm holding her and we're asleep in ten seconds."

"Julien Sorel would be impressed."

He smiled. "That was some feeling. Absolutely on empty. A little nap and we'll go again." He shook his head, leaned back in the chair to stretch. "Then, man, it's maybe 2:00 a.m. We're both asleep, lying buck naked on the sheets. There's a sound outside. I'm immediately awake. Look up. Make out a figure outside the window."

I laughed.

"Holy shit. Her Papa's caught on to us. I hear him talking to the *zamo*. He's coming after me."

I leaned back in my chair, grinning.

"Noiselessly, as the window's being raised, I pull the mosquito net from under the mattress. Her father climbs into the room and I slither out of bed onto the floor, hardly breathing. Then: What the hell? Guy's taking off his clothes. Not her father! He lifts the net on the other side and slides on top of Minou. I sit up and look. Some guy's jumping my Minou!"

I could not hide my amusement.

"You never saw ass pumping so hard. They both moan. Like she's never moaned for me! His head falls beside her, exhausted. He's smooching her face, her neck, her hair. I hear, *'Cara mia, adorata!'* It's that ugly dago priest!" He whispers, *'Adorata, adorata!'*" And am I PISSED!!!

"What'd you do?"

"What can I do? I slither around the bed, put on my pants. Or are they his? Who knows? Take all the clothes. Put on my shoes, take his. He's moaning, groaning, panting, suddenly snoring, and I'm out the window. Wave to the *zamo* and take off, laughing at the thought of that hypocrite! That bastard s'posed to be celibate! I think of him running with a horde of mosquitoes chasing his naked ass. I threw his clothes in the lake."

Minou came to the consul's house that night. Parks spoke to her outside. He returned ten minutes later, shook his head disgustedly at the colonel and me, but said nothing. It was quite a performance for a guy so given to expressing himself. He did not go out that night.

The next day Parks came again to my office. He paced back and forth. "That bitch!" he exclaimed. "Told me that had never happened before. She thought it was me until she heard that wop talk." He continued to pace. "Said she'd be more careful in the future who she confessed to and what she confessed." He stopped and shook his head. "Fuck her!" He resumed pacing. "Said it was my fault. Claimed I talked so much about her that any guy thought he could climb through her window." He kept pacing. "Bet for weeks she's been screwing that ugly priest. That whore!"

When he returned from Léo, the consul relaxed the no-roaming rules. He also advised us to be careful if we went out at night. He had heard from the Monsignor that recently when he'd been out making a mercy call on a parishioner, Père Nico had been stopped by drunk soldiers, stripped absolutely bare and left to walk back to the rectory naked.

A week or ten days later Parks saw Minou at the *Cercle Sportif.* They patched things up. He went adventuring again at night, but less frequently and never for more than a couple of hours. "I'm leaving the graveyard shift to the priest," he said.

If Parks had romantic troubles appropriate to the young, Colonel Bryant continued his liaison in a manner appropriate to the mature. He never mentioned the affair, but came out of it with a decent portrait of himself, a lion on one side, an elephant on the other.

Murielle

L ATE IN THE AFTERNOON AFTER COMING OUT of Parc Albert I left Charley and Paul Wemboyendja at the Hotel des Grands Lacs. I drove out of Goma to the nearby shantytown of Saké. I was hoping to find the turnoff to the DeMuncks' plantation and, if I was lucky, to meet them. While in Washington training for a Foreign Service assignment with USIS, I'd had the pleasure of meeting their daughter. It was improbable to encounter a young woman, a *colon*'s daughter, raised on a plantation in the Congo, then suffering such chaos. Even more improbable to fall in love with her. But she was a lovely person and I did.

In Washington I lived in the basement apartment in the home of the widow of an army general, a friend and classmate of General Eisenhower. He had been killed in a freak accident on a yacht in the Potomac River. Mrs Prichard was the mother of a classmate of mine at boarding school, but it was George DeGarmo who suggested that I share the basement apartment with him.

Serving as an officer at the Patuxent Naval Air Station in Maryland, George spent the week in his BOQ and the weekends in Washington. There he carried on a lively social life. George had been introduced into a Georgetown house full of young European women, mainly Belgian, although one of them was a Swede with that special charm for which Swedish girls had a reputation at that time. George and I used to hang around that house.

The Belgian girls had a friend working as an *au pair* for a naval architect living in McLean. Murielle often spent her free time at the house and we got to know her there. George took her out first, but there wasn't much rapport. I had been dating a diplomat's daughter with whom there was zero rapport. Once George moved on to Marcia, whom he later married, I was happy to try my luck with Murielle.

I had never dated a girl who was not an American. Murielle was both a European and not a European. When I first met her—in 1962—Americans knew nothing of Africa. They assumed it had no history. They thought it no surprise that men with joke-smith names—Lumumba,

Kasavubu, Tshombe—should make a mess of independence. And here was an attractive young woman who had grown up among these people. She had not been educated in the same way I had, but she spoke not only English, French and Swahili, but also a tribal language.

While I was receiving a thorough preparation for living overseas, she was already doing that—in America, looking out for herself, cut off from her family. For their safety her parents had sent their children off—she had several brothers—to Europe and America. The parents were trying to keep the plantation running in a Congo where change was constant and always uncertain.

Murielle was not beautiful in the way that American girls might be, having used the right soaps and cosmetics and hair dyes since high school. But she was pretty and carried herself well. She had a capacity to move around the world that I was only learning. I was very taken with her.

Murielle had enough experience with men not to treat them with the freedom Gunilla offered. Still, she was open to relationships. Being an *au pair* involved frustrations that made a young woman want outside contacts. I like to think that she sensed that I was a decent type, interested in friendship, a romance, but not in compromising her.

The first night I took her home, we parked outside the house in McLean for a long time, talking and getting to know one another, enjoying each other. We started dating.

Something else happened that spring. I got my overseas training assignment: Brussels, Belgium. Wow! Was this providential? I was already dating a Belgian girl.

I took her to movies. We went to plays, to a jazz club. I was earning decently and we had dinners in good restaurants. Sometimes we did things with the Belgian girls and their dates. One evening we went as a group to a dance place, patronized by black Americans. Oh, could they dance! During the competition we sat or stood at the edge of the dance floor. The others watched the dancers. I watched Murielle. I liked her more all the time.

The Belgian girls rented a house at Rehoboth Beach. One evening I drove Murielle there. On the way she lay down on the front seat, her head in my lap. (My brother and I had sometimes driven that way, back and forth from college.) At one point as we passed through a toll booth, the toll taker called to his partner, "Hey, d'you see that guy? There's a girl asleep on his lap!"

All spring I thought it wonderful to have found this friendship, to have a romance before going off to Europe. But what about when I left? I had never been good at playing at romance, knowing that the play always had to end. Was I thinking about some kind of future for this romance? Yes, I was. I liked this girl.

But I was also thinking about the trip George and Marcia and I were planning to take in France before I reported to Brussels. Marcia would have a college friend along for me. What about Murielle?

It may have been coming back from Rehoboth that Murielle and I talked about getting married. It could not have been very serious talk, but more serious than tentative beginnings like, "Do you ever think about marriage?" The possibility of marrying Murielle was certainly on my mind.

But unlike some men in my training class I would not rush into anything. They were trying to marry someone, anyone, fearful of encountering a foreign culture alone. My mother always contended that choosing to marry someone was the most important decision of one's life. So the decision demanded careful thought.

One night after being out, we came back to the basement apartment. We were alone. George was off at Patuxent and Mrs. Prichard had gone on a trip. We lay barefoot on my bed. It had the softest mattress I'd ever floated on. The air was cool in the dark room, but the summer night outside was warm. The slightest fragrance of Murielle's perfume made me dizzy, made me eager. The taste of her kisses made me think about our always being together.

I took off my shirt and invited her to take off hers. She did not move, said nothing, and gazed at the ceiling. I left the bed and took off my pants. I was now wearing only boxers. I suggested once again that she take off her top. She did not move. I embraced her.

I had always thought that steps forward in a romance should be matters of mutual agreement. I would not be a salesman of moving forward. I did not say, "You'll like it. You'll wonder why we haven't done this earlier. C'mon, Mu." I did not sell it, but I really wanted to hold her skin next to mine.

I pulled back from the embrace, nuzzling her, and asked, "Why not?" She said nothing. I kissed her. She whispered, "Because I'm Catholic." We pulled out of the embrace and stared at the ceiling.

Uh-oh. This sounded like serious Catholicism. That was why it was

As I drove to Saké, I passed the lava flow of Nyiragongo's most recent eruption. I drove down the only turn-off I could find. I passed mud-and-wattle huts . . .

so difficult to talk seriously about marriage, to negotiate what marriage would mean. I was willing to respect her religious beliefs, but I was not willing to be married in her church.

The Catholic Church at that time was not at all accommodating about adherents marrying outside the church. I regarded marrying in that church as a deal-breaker. I was afraid that priests would be part of the package. I did not want them inside my marriage.

I did not want my children raised in that faith. I was very leery of a Catholic girl telling me while we were courting that those things were not important to her, then deciding, after our children were born, that they were. I did not want my marriage or my children's upbringing to be pulled two different ways.

And so Murielle did not take off her top. She may not have refused because she was Catholic. It might have been because she was alone in a foreign country with no family to support her if she made a mistake. It may have been the assumption that removing one garment would only lead to removing others.

I might have said, "I love you. Let's talk about the actual possibility of our getting married. What do you think about that?"

And if she was agreeable to that, I might have said, "Would you be willing to marry me outside your church?"

But what if she said no? That was where I could not let this go. Because her refusal would mean the end of the romance.

So we lay on the bed, looking at the ceiling. The fragrance of her perfume faded away. The taste of her kisses no longer dazzled me. After a while we got off the bed. I put my pants back on.

Murielle was staying the night at the house. I took her up to the second floor and showed her into Mrs Prichard's guest room. I kissed her goodnight and went back downstairs.

I woke in the night and lay, thinking that if I were a real man I would tiptoe up to the guest room and get in bed with her. And what would happen would happen. But I was a guy waiting for a sign. She had chosen not to give it.

I have no memory of tearful goodbyes. I think perhaps the naval architect who turned out to be an officer with the CIA went on vacation with his family and took Murielle with them. At any rate the romance continued until that parting. It never had the closure of a break-up, of a discussion about what-happens-to-us-now.

Murielle went off. I joined George, Marcia, and Alison for sightseeing in Normandy. As a tourist I learned to play at faux romance with Alison. That's why we were together. So we enjoyed kisses on the side trails up Mont St Michel.

I suppose I wrote Murielle for a while from Belgium, but living in Europe was a new experience to savor and I savored it.

As I drove to Saké, I passed the lava flow of Nyiragongo's most recent eruption. I drove down the only turn-off I could find. I passed mud-and-wattle huts, asked directions of Congolese, received conflicting advice, and persevered. I came upon a locked gate. There I left the film truck. I climbed around the gate and walked to a plantation house constructed of lava blocks and set on a tall headland overlooking Lake Kivu.

It and the view were something out of movie versions of paradise. *South Pacific*'s Emile de Becque had a home like this and sang songs all day. How lucky the DeMuncks were to live here! But no one was around. I circled the house, wanting to verify that it was, indeed, the place where Murielle grew up. I determined that it was.

I had not seen Murielle in fifteen months. But already feeling the isolation of the Congo, already aware that there'd be no dating for me on this two-year tour, it was pleasant to think that a relationship with Murielle might still exist. The attraction between us had always been strong. Even if obstacles intruded, we really had loved each other. I left her parents a note.

I looked around at the view once more and returned to the gate. There I found a couple staring at the film truck. He wore khaki trousers and a tunic, belted, with pockets at the chest and below the belt. She looked very much like Murielle. I introduced myself, explaining that I was an American friend of their daughter, now living in Bukavu. I had no sense that either of them had ever heard of me. But why would Murielle have told them anything? What I did sense was that they were both enormously tired.

They invited me into the house. I felt uncomfortable at first, very aware that I was defying one of the fixed rules of my upbringing ("Never intrude!"). I was also conscious of the inadequacies of my French. But soon it was clear that the DeMuncks saw me as a pair of virgin ears. They could tell me things that their friends had grown tired of hearing.

Moreover, as an American officer, I represented that irresistible force, American policy, that they held responsible for much of the calamity that had befallen them. We had tea and a light supper.

Independence and its aftermath had turned their lives upside down, they said. Eighty percent of the workers on their coffee and tea plantations were Tutsis, originally from Rwanda, though they had lived in Congolese territory for generations. Now members of the Congolese government were threatening to force all Tutsis back into Rwanda.

When the DeMuncks had talked to North Kivu's provincial president—it clearly irked Madame to address him as "*Monsieur le Ministre*"—he had told them that if they supported the Tutsi work force, then they were "*contre*" the local government. "What can one do?" Madame asked.

She complained that local bandits were hired as police. These hoodlums terrorized the countryside, slitting the throats of plantation workers and beating pregnant women. I remembered Murielle telling me about plantation workers who had found the decapitated heads of fellow workers placed along footpaths.

"We sent the children outside the country," Madame said, "so they would be safe."

"We did not want them to see these things," Monsieur said.

"The children are safe," Madame went on, "but we have nothing to send them." That meant Murielle was on her own. She couldn't take chances with men, lying beside her on a summer night, wearing only boxers, who told her they loved her.

Monsieur explained that he had plowed all his money back into the plantation. He had put nothing away against a rainy day. "And why should I?" he asked. "In those days a Congolese franc was worth the same as a Belgian franc." Now the Congolese franc was worthless. Things kept breaking down. It was impossible to get spare parts and on a whim the government commandeered trucks.

Of course, they acknowledged, Belgium had lacked courage. To abandon the Congo in the manner it had! The Portuguese in Angola were right to hold on. And the Americans! Wasn't it clear that they intended to exploit the Congo's riches?

I listened as they let off steam. "*Mais vous ne dites rien!*" Madame kept saying. "You aren't saying anything!" But what was there to say?

I wondered what an American son-in-law's responsibilities would be to these good people so battered by the changes that independence had wrought. What would they be to Murielle's brothers? Where were those brothers? Were they faring as well as she was? *Au pair* was no long term arrangement.

At dinner I asked about Madame's photography. Murielle had told me about it. "There is no time anymore," she said. She caressed the dog with affection and conversed with the parrot. Monsieur chuckled now and then. I liked him for that. After dinner Madame showed me a collection of her photos printed as postcards. She stood behind me as I sat thumbing through them. Reminiscence warmed her voice.

When I said goodbye, they invited me to return. "Come spend a week," they suggested. "Climb our volcanoes. Or perhaps we could all go to Uganda. We know a place in Elizabeth Park. It's not usually open to tourists."

Driving back to Goma, I realized that I had not asked to see photos of Murielle as a child. I wondered if I would see them again. If I would see Murielle again. Or ever hear from her.

I did hear from her again. Almost a year later. After a long stint in another part of the Congo I had been reassigned to Bukavu, once again to direct the cultural center there, this time with some idea of what I was supposed to do. I must have written her several times to announce my return to the Kivu and my hopes of seeing her parents again. She was in Sterrbeck in Flemish Belgium. I was very ready now to rekindle the romance, very ready to hope that a young woman somewhere thought about me.

Her letter to me has disappeared. Mine to her still exists. It said:

Dear Murielle,

I've written you so many letters and sent them to so many crazy addresses and have appealed so many times to poor George and Marcia for news of you and have asked them to forward letters to you. . . All of which is to say that I don't know what you know about me and where you found it out. Since your letter arrived today addressed to Embassy Léopoldville, perhaps you got that address from Embassy Brussels.

For the moment I'm in Bukavu. I'm planning a trip up northwest of Goma where Rwandese refugee camps are located. I'll hope once again to see your parents. Are they still outside of Saké? I wrote you a week or so ago, again in the care of George and Marcia, but haven't written your parents. I'll have to work over a letter to them in a French that is more serviceable now than when you last saw me. Your letter will inspire me to action, particularly since I now have the correct address.

How do I like Africa? Well, I'm surviving. . . Now that the rains have begun, it's wetter here oftener than it ever was in Brussels. I came to like Belgium very much, by the way. Wish I were back there now. I'd pop over to Sterrbeck in Brabant. You're in Flanders, judging from *Tramlaan. Que veut dire ça?* (What does that mean?) *Avenue de Tram?*

I wish I could do something to get you to come down here. I'm quite serious when I say I can offer you a well-paying job here in my Cultural Center. We are looking for a European secretary-adminis-trator. Eighty-percent is convertible into Belgian francs. If this interests you, cable me (I'm not kidding) and reverse the charges. This is simply aggressive hiring practice.

At first I didn't know who your letter was from. (You aren't supposed to be in Belgium.) When I saw the Murielle, my heart beat faster; my blood pounded. After waiting so long for a letter, it was a reaction of delight mixed somehow with fear. You're terribly mysterious about explanations for silence, opening up "things have taken a long time to bury away." That means an unhappy love affair, I suppose. It depresses me to think of you unhappy. Especially when there is nothing I can do to change that unhappiness.

But what have you been doing, falling in love with somebody since I last saw you? You were supposed to be in love with me—or falling there. Why does a guy take a girl to Trader Vic's if she's not going to fall in love with him? Especially when he finds out (but realizes it too late) that he's gone and fallen in love with her! (Oh, that I should have realized that sooner and been able to tell you about it!) I hope, at any rate, that whatever it is that has been turning you into a woman of mystery and silence has dissolved.

Please let me hear from you. There's still a considerable soft spot in my heart for you (it could be melted again without difficulty) and I'd like us to forget the past months of silence and bridge the gap with some letters. Tell me what you are doing, where you are living, what sort of job you have. And I will try to get up to Goma to see your family.

Hooray! Since Murielle and I were suddenly back in contact, since my existence in the Congo no longer seemed entirely without the interest of a woman, I felt like a male being again.

I discovered that her parents were no longer at the plantation outside of Saké. Where had they gone? Had they left the Kivu? Just walked away from the life they had built there?

Then Paul Polakoff who worked with me at USIS Bukavu took a trip that included a foray into northern Rwanda. He went to see Rosamond Carr, a semi-legendary figure in that region. She was a pioneer, a divorced American woman living alone, who ran a pyrethrum farm. Pyrethrum flowers (Chrysanthemum), harvested mainly by African children who had nimbler fingers than their parents, served as the basic ingredient of natural insecticides.

When Paul returned, I asked, "Did you see Carr?"

"Amazing woman, living up there by herself, Rwanda's Karen Blixen."

"What's the farm like?"

"Beautiful country."

"A little lonely, I imagine."

He shrugged. "She reads a lot. There are pyrethrum bushes everywhere. Kids pick the flowers. Then they get vacuum-packed into large white sacks and sent off for processing."

"And no mosquitoes around."

"I didn't get bit." He started off, then turned back. "Say, I met some of her neighbors who say they know you."

"I don't know any people up there."

"A Belgian couple. M and Mme DeMunck."

"Really? They used to farm up near Goma. I visited them when I was here before."

"They showed me a note you'd written."

"Really?" Good heavens! They'd kept the note. "How was the French?"

"They appreciated the effort."

So the DeMuncks had moved to Rwanda. I wondered if they had left the Kivu permanently or were just waiting for things to stabilize, assuming that might actually happen.

Shortly afterwards I was in Goma, holding a series of film showings with Paul Wemboyendja. I shook free one afternoon after several morning shows in hopes of once again visiting the DeMuncks. I asked directions to Rosamond Carr's plantation, then asked around for directions to the DeMuncks.

Their house was small, a rustic, but rather charming cottage, high up in the volcano country. It stood on what struck me as a kind of moor, a stretch of green between ridges of hills, with heavy clouds pressing down against the country. It reminded me of Scotland and struck me as a depressing place, particularly after the splendor of the plantation house I had visited on the heights overlooking Lake Kivu.

But it was safer than the Kivu with less harassment from local officials. That was a real plus. Planters like them and Mrs Carr lived without any official protection at all. For their safety they had to rely on the good-will of the Africans in the neighborhood. Those neighbors were generally friendly and grateful for the work and wages the plantations provided. But independence had unsettled many things.

I admired the DeMuncks' tenacity in the face of all the reverses they had suffered. I wondered if tenacity was their only option. I wished I could have expressed that admiration to them face to face. Unfortunately, I learned that they had left for Kigali, the Rwandese capital, only four hours before I found their house. I left them a note.

A few weeks later a veritable road show descended upon us in Bukavu. The American Ambassador Mac Godley arrived with an entourage that included embassy officers as well as his sister and brother-in-law, both doctors in Massachusetts. The consul and I accompanied the group, first to Goma, then to Parc Albert where I saw my first lions, and lastly into Rwanda to visit Rosamond Carr.

The ambassador was divorced. As far as I could tell, it seemed to be embassy policy that a wife should be found for him. There were whispers that this was the reason for the visit to Mrs Carr. Her plantation lay beyond the ambassador's jurisdiction. I could not imagine why she would want to trade her quiet and fulfilling life to marry an ambassador. In fact, she didn't. The ambassador later married one of the embassy secretaries.

Given the size of our group, Mrs. Carr needed help preparing for us. Although they had disappeared when we arrived, the DeMuncks provided that help. While the others toured Mrs Carr's holding, I slipped off to see if I could once again find the cottage where I had missed them by a few hours.

Yes, they remembered me. We greeted each other like old friends. We had tea together. I was grateful that after eighteen months of non-stop usage my French had much improved. "And where is Murielle these days?" I asked. "I got a letter from her not too long ago. She was in Belgium."

"She's back in America now," said Madame. "In Washington."

"With a job," said Monsieur.

"Living with two young women."

"Could I have her address?" I asked. "My tour here ends in two or three months. I'll be in Washington. Maybe I can see her."

When Madame gave me her address, I asked about the DeMuncks' removal to Rwanda. Was it permanent?

"No, we expect to go back," said Madame. "But it's a great relief to be here for a while without all the interference of officials."

"We will go back one day," her husband assured me. "We can't stay away. But a little rest is welcome."

I asked about the other children. One of the sons was talking about returning to help run the plantation. Hanging on was what most of the Belgians still around were trying to do. Some had no other options. Some lacked the courage to start again—and, in any case, where would they start? Some of them loved Africa and would hold on as long as they could. The DeMuncks fell into this last category.

On my earlier visit I had found the couple frustrated and worn out. I was very pleased this time that they were rested and in good humor. I could not stay long lest my absence be noticed and disapproved by my immediate boss, the Bukavu consul. I said goodbye and thanked them for their hospitality.

As soon as I returned to Bukavu, I wrote Murielle that I had seen them. I said I hoped I would see her when I came through Washington.

When I returned to Washington, seeing Murielle was the top priority on my list. We had been writing back and forth, not too frequently and mainly as friends. But I thought of her every day. I felt certain the attraction we felt for one another was still very strong. I wondered if it might be best to stop worrying about all that we had never discussed before. She had written with a little pique that I had asked her to marry me the way a Congolese would ask. I was not sure what that meant, but clearly it was no compliment. Maybe now I should lay the offer on the table like a go-ahead American, put some sales pitch behind it, and leave religious negotiations until after we were married.

Before seeing her, I checked in at USIA. I had been reassigned as the USIS youth officer in Karachi, Pakistan. That sounded interesting, a new part of the world to learn about and explore. It would be wonderful to live there with Murielle at my side.

Unfortunately, however, I did not feel that I understood about Africa in much depth and about what American policy was trying to do there. I sometimes felt that we Americans were running the Congo without understanding the society and how it worked. I wondered if Foreign Service life was a matter of living in many places without deeply understanding any of them. And I wondered if going out again unmarried was a good idea. If nothing could be worked out with Murielle, it might be best to resign.

I saw Murielle after work. Unfortunately, she was busy that evening. Of course, I was nervous, but once I embraced her, the nervousness was gone. We went to a restaurant to have tea and sat at a table outside. We started talking as if we had never been apart. That very strong attraction between us was still there. We both felt it. I saw Murielle trying to resist its pull—maybe that was not unwise—but I grinned at her and said, "Don't fight it. How great it is to see you!"

We chatted along: how did she like her job? Who were her housemates? How had she found them? Did they all get along? We reminisced about the house the Belgians girls had and the good times there. What had happened to those girls? I had escorted one of them to her brother's wedding in Brussels. I told Murielle about seeing her parents. A brother, she said, had already returned to help his father rehabilitate the plantation at Saké. I talked about the work I had done in the Congo, about my doubts about American policy. I said I was slated to go to Karachi. What kind of a place would that be?

"Smelly," she said, laughing. "Crowded." She suddenly spoke in an

Indian accent that she might have picked up from an Asian *wallah* somewhere. "You will be very happy in Karachi, sahib."

We laughed together. I looked across the table at her. "Do you want to come to Karachi with me?" The smile faded from her face. "I mean it," I said. "Why don't you come to Karachi with me?"

She pulled back. "There's something I must tell you."

"Don't pull away. There's a very strong attraction here. Don't pretend it doesn't exist. That you don't feel it."

She looked down at her teacup. "I'm engaged to be married." She raised the cup to her lips and drank.

I drank some tea long enough to absorb this news. "What does that have to do with anything?" I asked. "You're having tea with an old friend. He's loved you for a long time and wants only what's best for you. And he thinks what's best is that you come with him to Karachi."

She gazed at me for a long time without speaking. I gazed back. I had seen this happen in movies: a man and a woman gazing into each other's souls. But it had never happened to me. It was happening now.

"Even if it's smelly," I said at last. "Even if it's crowded." I reached across the table to take her hand. She withdrew it and shook her head. I attempted the Indian accent. "You could be very happy in Karachi, *memsa'b*."

"You have a terrible accent."

"In several languages. I'm told I speak French with a Congolese accent."

"Ooo!" she said with a smile. "I must go."

"Don't run away from this, Mu. I've been thinking about you for months."

"I'm expected for dinner. I must go."

She stood and started toward the sidewalk. I took her wrist to stop her. "Meet me tomorrow. Same time, same place." She shook her head. "I love you. This is your life. You know what my mother says about—"

"I know what she says."

"I'll wait for you tomorrow."

She shook her head and hurried away from me along the sidewalk. I went back onto the terrace to pay the bill. I went to the car I'd rented—at first I couldn't remember what kind of car I'd gotten—and drove to Mrs Prichard's house. I was staying again in the basement.

The next day I went to a market and got some things to feed her. I did not want us to be in a public place. There must have been something about feeding her that said, "I can take care of you. I want to take care of you."

I parked near her office, uncertain that she would come. That days' nervousness was exponentially worse than that of the day before. At the hour I'd met her the day before she did not come. Was she testing me? Or had she been forced to stay late? Or was she wrestling with herself?

Finally I saw her coming along the sidewalk. I hurried up to her, put my arm around her and, although she did not want to let me, I kissed her cheek. "What a coincidence," I said, "I just got here myself."

"Liar. I've been watching you for twenty minutes."

"Caught out. You look fantastic today!"

"This old rag?"

I laughed. "We're both liars."

I put her in the car and explained that for tea I was taking her to a place she knew. When I pulled up in front of Mrs Prichard's house, she gazed at it and finally asked, "Is this the place I stayed that night?"

I took her around to the side entrance to the basement apartment. I had set up a table for our tea and put hors d'oeuvres and cheese and bread before her. I readied the tea. I tried to make conversation, asking Murielle questions. She hardly spoke.

I made conversation while we ate. Eventually she relaxed. She had been resisting the attraction between us, as if she could resist the weather or hold back the tides. She gave into it enough not to resist it. I drew my chair up next to hers. I leaned forward, took her head in my hands, and kissed her. She tried to resist it, shaking her head, but the kiss made us both lightheaded.

"Let's go right now," I said, "right now! And get a marriage license."

She was silent for a time, then said, "Everything's closed."

"Then we'll go tomorrow." I looked deeply into her eyes and once more we gazed at each other in that way I had never done with anyone else. "Stay here tonight."

She shook her head.

"Tomorrow we'll get a marriage license and your clothes and we'll go somewhere during the waiting period. Then we'll come back and get married and go to Pakistan together."

She shook her head, smiling. "You're crazy," she said, laughing.

"Let's go somewhere right now. There's plenty of money. I've gotten hardship pay for two years."

She kept shaking her head.

"We can check into a motel as a married couple and tomorrow buy you everything new from the skin out."

"I've got to go," she said, laughing.

"I'm not joking. I love you. I'm offering you a life. Don't resist this incredible attraction between us. You're here because you know it's real."

"I do know it's real," she said. "I've been thinking about Pakistan. But can I just walk out on my life?"

"I'll make sure you never regret it."

"Please take me back." She stood up and smoothed her dress. I did not move. "Please. I'm meeting someone for dinner. I can't not go." To get me on my feet, she offered, "I'll see you again tomorrow."

I stood. "I'll come at noon. We'll get a license."

I drove her to the place where I'd met her. When I stopped the car at the sidewalk, she said, "Come again at 4:30."

"I'll come at noon." I leaned over to kiss her. She shook her head and was gone. I watched her hurry down the sidewalk and turn in at the building where she worked.

I was supposed to have dinner that evening with George and Marcia. They did not know I was seeing Murielle. They wanted to introduce me to women I might like and some friend Marcia had known at college was joining us for dinner. I would be expected to drive her home, kiss her goodnight in the car, maybe do some necking if we'd hit it off, even some petting, and ask her out the next night. But I was an emotional wreck.

"What's wrong?" George asked.

"I'm having trouble handling American life."

George and Marcia drove the friend home. I paced a while in their apartment. Finally I wrote them a note, thanking them for dinner, and went home to clean up the remains of tea in the basement apartment.

The next day I went to meet Murielle at noon. I waited till 1:30. She didn't come. She arrived promptly at 4:30. We walked to a nearby park, a small urban square with some benches. When we sat down, she did not look at me. "I can't see you again," she said. "I'm going out of town tonight." It was Friday. "To Rehoboth Beach. I won't be back till Monday."

"We went there together," I said.

She nodded and finally looked at me. Again we held each other's eyes.

She had to feel that power between us. It was why she was there. "I was up all night," she said. "Thinking about us and running off and Pakistan." Her eyes were shining with what might become tears. "I just can't do that. Part of me wants to, I don't deny that. But I just can't."

I took her hand. She pulled it away.

"I can't see you again. Ever." She almost visibly took command of herself. She stood. "I'm going now. You mustn't come with me."

"I—"

"You say you love me. Then let me go alone."

I took her upper arms. "May I kiss you?"

"No. I don't want to cry and I will."

She turned from me and walked off. I watched her till she turned the corner.

When it got to be early evening, I went over to George and Marcia's. They welcomed me in. "Are you feeling better now?" George asked.

"I'm terribly sorry about the way I behaved last night. Your friend was very nice. I'm sorry I was so rude to her."

"She did wonder," Marcia said, "why a guy who hadn't dated a white woman in two years refused to take her home."

"I'm out of practice, I guess. Afraid I'd make a fool of myself."

"I'm afraid we made some jokes about you in the car," George said. "We'll pay you the compliment of not repeating them."

"Can I take you two to dinner?" I asked.

We agreed on a place we could walk to in Georgetown. Marcia called for a reservation.

When she came back, I said, "For the past three days I've been trying to persuade Murielle DeMunck to marry me."

"So that's what was going on."

"This time yesterday I thought she might say yes."

"Isn't she engaged?" Marcia asked.

"That's why she said no."

"Don't worry," said George. "The woods are full of young women wanting to go to Karachi. And you have three weeks to find one."

I resigned from USIS and returned home to Los Angeles. As a way both to understand better what I'd experienced in the Congo and to adjust to American life, I enrolled in a masters degree program in African Studies at UCLA. I also spent time in the Theater Arts department; to stay sane I had written plays in the Congo. During that time I met the daughter of a recently retired Foreign Service officer and we were married. After getting my degree I stumbled into a job as a correspondent covering Africa— our son was born in Nairobi—and covered the continent for four years. I never returned to the Congo. Once I returned to the paper's Boston offices, a play of mine found a small measure of success, enough to lead me out of journalism into screenwriting.

For a time I felt a terrible nostalgia for Africa. But time heals everything. I rarely thought of Murielle. But now and then I'd see a woman who reminded me of her and I'd think: "How strong that attraction was!"

After he retired from USIS, Paul Polakoff settled in Los Angeles where he grew up. We stayed in touch. He had married his college sweetheart, in Bukavu of all unlikely places. They had lost track of one another. Claire had married, had two daughters, and divorced their father. Paul's mother got Paul and her back together and maneuvered the African wedding.

After retiring, Paul served as a guide for Francophone African visitors to America. He kept in touch with people he had known during a career that took him as an Africa specialist all over the continent.

One evening we met for dinner at a restaurant. We talked Africa and travel, what Claire's kids were doing in college and ours was doing in grammar school. Eventually we said goodbye, promising to get together again before too long.

When the ladies left the restaurant, Paul took me aside. "You're the one who knew a couple named DeMunck. Isn't that right? I met them up in Rwanda."

"Yes," I said. "I snuck off to see them when Mac Godley was wooing— What was her name?"

"Rosamond Carr? I met them when I went to see her."

"I think they expected to go back to—"

"Yes, they did." Paul looked at me with a strange expression. I was sure he recalled that I had a special regard for the DeMuncks. "They went back to the plantation they had south of Goma."

"A son was going to help them work it," I said.

"Yes, he did." A pause, then: "A couple of weeks ago the father and son were killed."

"No!" I felt a hollowness in my guts. "What in the world happened?"

"They had gone to Goma to get funds to pay workers their monthly wages. Thieves knew they had gone there. They waited on the road back to the farm. I guess they set up a roadblock." Paul shrugged. "When DeMunck stopped the car, thieves ran out of the bush. Dragged both men from their car and killed them. Made off with the cash."

I thought of Murielle. Poor woman!

"I knew the DeMunck daughter in Washington. Jesus!"

Paul and I went outside where our wives were chatting. "Sorry to be the bearer of bad news," he said. "But I thought you'd want to know."

"Yes. Thank you for telling me."

As we drove home, I was unusually quiet. "Anything wrong?" asked my wife.

"Polakoff just told me that some people I knew in the Kivu were murdered."

"How terrible!"

"It's such a beautiful place. But so cruel."

Driving on, I thought: What good people the DeMuncks were. How pointless to kill those men. A bit of money for a time. But all those jobs lost.

I wondered what Mme DeMunck would do now. Go back to Belgium? And what about the son's wife? There must have been a wife. Possibly children. And I wondered about Murielle.

Oh, Murielle! Dear Murielle. How I wish I could console you!

Afterword

Introduction

My experience in Coquilhatville, opening a cultural center alone in the remote Equateur region of the Congo, is detailed in my memoir Equateur: A Year at the Edge of the Jungle.

See-Nay-Ma

Belgium's only colony, the Belgian Congo, acceded to independent nationhood on June 30, 1960. The Belgians and the Congolese had differing expectations about what independence would bring. Many Belgians expected that little would change. Most Congolese assumed independence would mean that Africans would become equal citizens with colonials. When this failed to materialize, Congolese workers walked off their jobs. When Force Publique officers acted as if nothing had changed, the soldiers under their command mutinied. Public order collapsed. Many former colonials fled. The United Nations sent peacekeepers to the Congo, its first attempt to restore order in a country where chaos had broken out. They entered the country July 15, 1960.

When I arrived in the Congo on August 1, 1963, the Congo had been independent just three years. A kind of order had been restored, but UN peacekeepers were still holding things together.

Under Belgian colonial administration, the colony had been divided into six provinces. The Kivu was the province in the farthest east of the country. Bukavu served as its capital. In 1963 those administrative provinces remained in place. Eventually they would completely changed.

Shortly after independence Katanga, the province directly south of the Kivu, attempted to secede. Katanga comprised the rich mining area of the copper belt, a region that had poured vast wealth into Belgium. Its Congolese rulers, advised by former Belgian administrators, sought unsuccessfully to retain the old order. The secession lasted into 1965.

Playing Toulouse

The American Consulate in Bukavu was led by the consul, whom I have called Carl Hillis, not his real name. He took care of State Department functions: political reporting and consular activities. Also working at the consulate was the representative of the Central Intelligence Agency (CIA) whose functions included intelligence matters. At this time a primary intelligence concern was to keep tabs on how countries of the Communist Bloc would try to gain influence in Central Africa. Down the hill from the consulate was the cultural center of the United States Information Service (USIS). It included a library and a film service.

The American presence at this time included an embassy in the capital Leopoldville (now Kinshasa) and consulates, including State Department, CIA and USIS officers, at Elisabethville (now Lubumbashi) in the Katanga, Stanleyville (now Kisangani) in Orientale province, and Bukavu in the Kivu. The embassy would soon send USIS officers to establish American Cultural Centers in Coquilhatville (now Mbandaka) in Equateur province (where I was sent) and in Luluabourg (now Kananga) in the Kasai.

Home schooling. I do not remember—if I ever knew—what the Hillises did about schooling their two boys. It's very likely that Harriet Hillis home-schooled them. This meant that the Hillis boys had little opportunity to forge friendship with other children. What friendships they might have had would have been with the children of the colonials who remained in Bukavu.

The Future and the Past
Social activities were an important way for the American consul to make contacts and learn what was going on in the Kivu. These included the kind of men's lunch, described in this reminiscence, as well as holding "cocktails" (as they were called) in the late afternoon/early evening and dining guests of all sorts, including Americans passing through.

This outreach included getting to know people doing a variety of things: American missionaries, of course, and others. I remember accompanying the Hillises on a visit to the Institut de la Recherche Scientifique en Afrique Centrale. It was run by a scientist considered an important member of the Kivu community.

The UN flew food and other aid into isolated and needy communities. Local people well knew that a circling white plane meant that UN aid was arriving.

Positively Curvaceous
Bukavu was built on five peninsulas stretching into the south end of Lake

Kivu. Hills rose abruptly behind the town. So there was no land on which an airport could be built. Kamembe Airport serving Bukavu was located across the international border in small Rwanda town of Cyangugu. As I recall, Kamembe was built on a ridge of land long enough to accommodate a landing strip. But it was situated on the ridge in a way that complicated landings. Not a pilot, I can't say exactly what the problem was. Except I recall that it was easy to misjudge the landing by coming in too low. The Bukavu CIA officer did this once, crashing his small plane before reaching the runway. Fortunately, he survived the crash.

In the colonial days and the years immediately following, a number of well-heeled Belgians lived in Bukavu. So it was possible for the American consuls to employ very good cooks to prepare their meals. And it was, of course, a happy circumstance to have a good cook—who would also do the marketing—if your job required a good deal of entertaining.

The Prince Sees the Mwami

Mark Stern (the name has been changed) was able to write and file a piece about his interview with the Mwami of Kabare that never happened. As I recall, it did appear well back in the paper next to department store ads.

Correspondents from Mark's paper were customarily accorded extraordinary service from Americans in the field, more than other news media. Those correspondents really were treated rather like princelings. A positive report could not possibly damage an officer's career; a name mentioned was a definite plus. A negative report could hurt an officer's career. A correspondent's grumbling that he had not been given needed help might at the least result in a tsk-tsk or a reprimand.

Kivu Safari

The then splendid Hotel des Grands Lacs still exists, but has fallen on hard times as has Goma itself. Says Lonely Planet: "Once Goma's grandest hotel, this colonial relic's grandeur has certainly failed, but its rooms are a great deal given their central location. The apartments have air-con, while wi-fi is only in the restaurant."

Parc National Albert has now been renamed Virunga National Park. Ruindi Camp apparently still exists; Vitshumbi Fishing Camp as well. For decades the Congo has not been able to give the park the resources and attention it needs. The Rwandan massacres of the mid-'90s destabilized the entire area. Guerrilla groups menace the area. They have hunted the animals for food. Consulting the park website a visitor is told: "Virunga needs your financial support now."

Bukavu Again

In late 1964 I returned to Bukavu, once again on temporary duty as the USIS PAO (Public Affairs Officer). After leaving there some fifteen months earlier, I had, working alone, established the American post, a cultural center, at Coquilhatville in Equateur Province. The cultural center there had been slow starting; it seemed to take forever to get the needed supplies shipped up the Congo River from Leopoldville. Once the center was open and operating, the Simba Rebellion, which started farther east, began to threaten Coq. When the rebels were only hours outside the town, I was ordered to evacuate the post. Although the rebels never actually entered Coq, the post was not reopened.

After my time in the isolated Coquilhatville, it was a kind of heaven to be back in the Kivu. The climate was benign, there were friendships to be had, the USIS operation was well in hand, it was possible to take film trips at least around Lake Kivu.

Jack Parks

Since the local commander of the ANC (*Armee Nationale Congolaise*) regarded himself highly after repelling a rebel attack on Bukavu, he did not want—nor felt he needed—the military advice of an American Lieutenant Colonel. I never really figured out what Bryant and Parks (the names have been changed) did in Bukavu except pleasure selected ladies of the community.

As I was about to leave the Kivu and Africa, I ordered a Karmann Ghia sports sedan from Gaillard. I picked it up in Belgium, drove it south across France to Nice where it was loaded onto the liner on which I crossed the Atlantic. (It may have been the United States Lines since we were required to use American-owned transportation.) The journey across the Atlantic was a good way to shed some of the effects of Africa. I drove the car across the States to Los Angeles and felt proud of it since the Karmann Ghia was rarely seen in the States.

Headed back to Africa five years later, my wife Donanne and I drove that car back across the States. About to leave for Nairobi, I found the car difficult to sell on the East Coast where the Ghia model was unknown. Finally I drove it into a used car dealership, told the owner that I was leaving the next day for Africa and implored him to take the car off my hands, which he did, getting a very good deal.

At the time the C-47 crew was overflying the mountains south of Bukavu, Laurent Kabila, the figurehead leader of the ragtag army that overthrew Mobutu, was living among rebels in those mountains.

Murielle

I never heard from or about Murielle after she left me that day in the park. I assume she married her fiancé and I hope lived happily ever after.

When I was in Bukavu, Rosamund Carr was a legendary figure there, living on a pyrethreum farm north of Gisenyi, Rwanda. She was then in her early 50s. Her death at 94 in 2006 evoked this short notice on the internet: "Rosamond Carr, a Manhattan fashion illustrator whose love affair with Africa long survived her divorce from the dashing big-game hunter she followed there and culminated when she, as an octogenarian, opened an orphanage in war-ravaged Rwanda." She wrote *Land of a Thousand Hills: My Life in Rwanda* with Anne Howard Halsey.

Paul Polakoff served with me at USIS Bukavu, preparing the daily news bulletin, drawn from Voice of America radio broadcasts, that served as a kind of newspaper in Bukavu. He belonged to the Table Ronde in Bukavu, a men's club much like the Lions Club. He started his Foreign Service career doing staff jobs at the American Embassy in Paris, later transferring to USIS.

When I first knew him, in his early to mid-30s and unmarried, I assumed Paul was destined to remain a bachelor as long as he served in Africa. This was a fate I myself wanted to avoid; it led to my resignation from USIS. Thus it was much to my astonishment when I leaned that, thanks to his mother's intervention, he had married his college sweetheart. As I recall, he and Claire (who was divorced and had two daughters) married on an island in Lake Kivu. I always wondered if they had any time to reacquaint themselves with each other. Or did Claire just trust her memory, take her two daughters to Bukavu and marry the man?

After Paul left the Foreign Service, he and Claire settled in Los Angeles where they had gone to school (UCLA). Speaking excellent French, Paul hosted State Department Francophone visitors on their trips around the United States. We saw each other with some regularity. After Claire's passing, he married Phyline. He passed on in 2015.

Naming

Some historians group under the name "Simba" the many small and large rebellions instigated through the Congo from 1963 to 1965. As this newly independent nation fought internally to establish power relationships, it also worked externally to elicit aid from one side or the other in the Cold War.

Note also that the "ANC" in this book refers to the *Armée Nationale Congolaise.* This is the army of the Congolese government, not the rebels. It is not the political party with the same acronym associated with Nelson Mandela in South Africa.

This book concerns the Democratic Republic of the Congo, sometimes referred to as Congo-Kinshasa, DR Congo, the DRC, the DROC or simply the "Congo." Before 1997 it was called "Zaire."

Books by Frederic Hunter

Africa Africa!: Fifteen Stories (Cune Press, 2000).
The Girl Ran Away: A Story from Africa (Cune Press, 2014).
*Kivu: Journeys in Eastern Congo in a Time of Rebellion
    and Cold War* (Cune Press, 2022).

Forthcoming from Cune Press:
Congo Prophet: A Novel (Fall, 2022).
Madagascar and Other Stories (Winter, 2023).
Joss the Ambassador's Wife: A Novel (Spring, 2023).
The Late Middle Age of Kwame Johnson: A Novel (Fall, 2023).
Equateur: A Year at the Edge of the Jungle (Spring, 2024).
Dinner in Ouagadougou (Fall, 2024)

Credits for Illustrations

1 Map of Africa   7   Gary Albright Design.
2 Map of Congo   8   Gary Albright Design.
3 Map of Kivu region   9   Gary Albright Design.
4 Fred Hunter, Congo 1963   14 Frederic Hunter Collection.
5 The American Consulate in Bukavu   16   Frederic Hunter Collection.
6 Sim to Bukavu consul's residence   22   Dreamstime 51725776 © Askme9.
7 Unloading Boats 29 Dreamstime 19513406 © Antonella865.
8 Baby Elephant   35   Dreamstime 77661402 © Andrey Gudkov.
9 Mountains   39   Dreamstime 114474375 © Perambulator.
10 Mountains, Islands   56   Dreamstime 49746448 © Hagen Berndt.
11 Pirogues   58   Dreamstime 19513371 ©Antonella865.
12 Kudu (Antelope)   62   Dreamstime 203530417 © Jim808080.
13 Hippos   65   Dreamstime 90643585 © Lianquan Yu.
14 A Pretty Woman   67   iStock 1227595864 © Fotografia, Inc.
15 Forest Elephant   69   Dreamstime 77661754 © Andrey Gudkov.
16 Roan Antelope   71   Dreamstime 710337 © Ecophoto.
17 Fish from Lake Kivu   73   Dreamstime 32868123 ©Hagen Berndt.
18 Shanties near Saké   80   Dreamstime 33276196 © Jagem Berndt.
19 C-47 (spy plane)   90   Dreamstime 6978030 © Joseph Ceschin.
20 Bedroom Window   93   Dreamstime 229072316 © Benjawan Sittidech.
21 C -130 Hercules   95   iStock 521932967 © photographicsolutionsuk
22 Mt Nyiragongo   102   Dreamstime 139722584 ©Eokwong.
23 Cover   Dreamstime 114474192 © Perambulator.

Further Reading

Achebe, Chinua. *Things Fall Apart* (Penguin Books , 1994).

Ba, Mariama. *So Long a Letter* (Waveland Press, 2012).

Blixen, Karen (aka Isak Dinesen). *Out of Africa* (Modern Library, 1992).

Camara Laye. *The Dark Child* (Farrar, Straus and Giroux, 1954).

Coetzee, J. M. *Disgrace* (Penguin Books, 2000).

Conrad, Joseph, *Heart of Darkness (1899).*

Dinesen, Isak (Karen Blixen), *Out of Africa (Modern Library, 1992).*

Eggers, Dave, *What Is the What* (McSweeney's, 2006).

The Autobiography of Valentino Achak Deng, (Vintage Books, 2007).

Emecheta, Buchi. *The Joys of Motherhood* (George Braziller Inc, 2013).

Gordimer, Nadine. *A World of Strangers* (Penguin Books, 1984).

Hemingway, Ernest. *The Green Hills of Africa* (Scribner, 2016).

Kingsolver, Barbara. *The Poisonwood Bible* (Harper Perennial, 2008).

Mandela, Nelson, *Long Walk to Freedom (*Little, Brown, Boston, 1994).

Markham, Beryl, *West with the Night (*North Point Press, 1983).

Mathabane, Mark. *Kaffir Boy* (Free Press, 1998).

Merriam, Alan P., *Congo: Background of Conflict (Northwestern Uni Press, 1961).*

Naipaul, V. S. *A Bend in The River* (Vintage, 1989).

Ngugi wa Thiong'o. *Petals of Blood* (Penguin Classics, 2005).

Reader, John, *Africa: A Biography of the Continent*, (Vintage Books, 1999).

Van Reybrouck, David. *Congo: The Epic History of A People* (Ecco, 2015).

Index

CUNE PRESS WAS FOUNDED in 1994 to publish thoughtful writing of public importance. Our name is derived from "cuneiform." (In Latin *cuni* means "wedge.")

In the ancient Near East the development of cuneiform script—simpler and more adaptable than hieroglyphics—enabled a large class of merchants and landowners to become literate. Clay tablets inscribed with wedge-shaped stylus marks made possible a broad inter-meshing of individual efforts in trade and commerce.

Cuneiform enabled scholarship to exist, art to flower, and created what historians define as the world's first civilization. When the Phoenicians developed their sound-based alphabet, they expressed it in cuneiform.

The idea of Cune Press is the democratization of learning, the faith that rarefied ideas—pulled from dusty pedestals and displayed in the streets—can transform the lives of ordinary people. And it is the conviction that ordinary people, trusted with the most precious gifts of civilization, will give our culture elasticity and depth—a necessity if we are to survive in a time of rapid change.

Aswat: Voices from a Small Planet (a series from Cune Press)

Looking Both Ways	Pauline Kaldas
Stage Warriors	Sarah Imes Borden
Stories My Father Told Me	Helen Zughraib

 Syria Crossroads (a series from Cune Press)

Leaving Syria	Bill Dienst & Madi Williamson
Visit the Old City of Aleppo	Khaldoun Fansa
The Dusk Visitor	Musa Al-Halool
Steel & Silk	Sami Moubayed
Syria - A Decade of Lost Chances	Carsten Wieland
The Road from Damascus	Scott C. Davis
A Pen of Damascus Steel	Ali Ferzat
White Carnations	Musa Rahum Abbas

 Bridge Between the Cultures (a series from Cune Press)

Confessions of a Knight Errant	Gretchen McCullough
Afghanistan & Beyond	Linda Sartor
Apartheid is a Crime	Mats Svensson
The Passionate Spies	John Harte
Congo Prophet	Frederic Hunter
Music Has No Boundaries	Rafique Gangat

Cune   Cune Press: www.cunepress.com

FREDERIC HUNTER SERVED as a Foreign Service Officer in the United States Information Service in Brussels, Belgium, and, shortly after its independence, at three posts in the Republic of the Congo: Bukavu, Coquilhatville, and Léopoldville. He later became the Africa Correspondent of the *Christian Science Monitor*, based in Nairobi.

A playwright / screenwriter, Hunter's award-winning stage work, The *Hemingway Play*, was given a reading at the Eugene O'Neill Playwrights Conference, presented at Harvard University's Loeb Drama Center and produced by PBS's Hollywood Television Theater series. Other plays have been performed at the Dallas Theatre Center, ACT in San Francisco, and the Ensemble Theater in Santa Barbara.

Movies Hunter has written have been produced by PBS, ABC, and CBS. Research for his PBS drama *Lincoln and the War Within* led him to write the historical novel *Abe and Molly: The Lincoln Courtship*. He's taught screenwriting at the Santa Barbara Writers Conference, at UCSB, and at Principia College where he also taught Modern African Literature. Hunter's Africa experience is the basis for ten current and forthcoming novels and short story collections from Cune Press.

Fred Hunter blogs at www.TravelsinAfrica.com.

CPSIA information can be obtained
at www.ICGtesting.com
Printed in the USA
JSHW020953070322
23556JS00003B/4